Please Don't Cry

**A family torn apart by grief.
An incredible act of love.**

JANE PLUME

Virgin BOOKS

2 4 6 8 10 9 7 5 3 1

First published in 2014 by Virgin Books,
an imprint of Ebury Publishing

A Random House Group Company

Copyright © Jane Plume 2014

Jane Plume has asserted her right under the Copyright, Designs and
Patents Act 1988 to be identified as the author of this work.

Every reasonable effort has been made to contact copyright holders
of material reproduced in this book. If any have inadvertently been
overlooked, the publishers would be glad to hear from them and make
good in future editions any errors or omissions brought to their attention.

Addresses for companies within The Random House Group Limited can
be found at www.randomhouse.co.uk/offices.htm

The Random House Group Limited Reg. No. 954009

A CIP catalogue record for this book is available from the British Library

The Random House Group Limited supports the Forest Stewardship
Council® (FSC®), the leading international forest-certification organisation.
Our books carrying the FSC label are printed on FSC®-certified paper.
FSC is the only forest-certification scheme supported by the leading
environmental organisations, including Greenpeace. Our paper
procurement policy can be found at
www.randomhouse.co.uk/environment

Printed and bound by CPI Group (UK) Ltd, Croydon, CR0 4YY

ISBN: 9780753555385

To buy books by your favourite authors and register for offers,
visit www.randomhouse.co.uk

To Marco, Millie, Lewis, Ashton & Anni-Mae
~ Quite simply, my world ~

CONTENTS

PROLOGUE

Tuesdays had always been my least favourite day. Tuesday was evening surgery at the medical centre where I worked, and that meant it would be past eight o'clock before I got home to the kids.

On 12 October 2010 at 12.30 p.m., I arrived at the clinic as usual.

'Hopefully it will be quiet later,' I remember thinking, 'so I can give Gina a call.'

She was my best friend and we were planning one of our regular 'girly nights' that Friday, which meant face masks, pedicures and too much wine. It would end up messy, with us giggling like a couple of school kids. I couldn't wait.

Shortly after two, my mobile phone rang and the caller display told me that it was Gina's mum. My first thought was, 'Why on earth would Gina's mum be ringing me at work?'

I picked up the phone. 'Hello, you,' I said, in a light-hearted, breezy voice.

Nothing could have prepared me for what I was about to hear.

PART ONE

CHAPTER 1

THE START OF A
BEAUTIFUL FRIENDSHIP

'You'd love Gina, one of the girls I work with,' my
old friend Hayley said to me over a cup of coffee
one lunchtime. 'She's mad as a hatter, just like you.
I reckon you'd get on like a house on fire.'

It was 2000 and I was working as a clinical
studies coordinator for the pharmaceutical company
AstraZeneca in Loughborough, and I loved my job.
Don't get me wrong, the work was intense, at times
difficult, and the hours, combined with the fact that
I had recently become a single mum to Marco and
Millie – then aged six and four – following a split
from my husband, meant that my life was hectic.
But I was happy and had the support of my family
and some really good friends.

Hayley was one of these friends. I had known her since she was 16 and she had been my bridesmaid at my wedding. She also worked for AstraZeneca, though at a different site. It wasn't the first time she had mentioned Gina, and she wasn't the only one. I had heard the name Gina Hibberd mentioned by various other colleagues and I remembered seeing a site-wide email when she got married a few years before, so I knew she was a PA in another department but I had never spoken to her and didn't really give the conversation much thought after that.

A few days later, Gina came up to the clinical studies department and as soon as she walked in the door I knew who she was from the way our colleagues had described her. I heard her before I saw her and, to be honest, my initial thought was 'The gob on that! God, she's loud'. When Hayley had described Gina to me, she had told me a couple of times, 'You can't miss her smile.' She was so right; Gina had the biggest, widest, most genuine smile I had ever seen. It really did light up the room. Apart from her loud voice, it was the first thing that struck you. She was quite tall, compared to my five foot two inches at least, and in her heels she seemed to dwarf me. She had lovely shoulder-length shiny chocolate-brown hair and big brown eyes. On that occasion, Gina was smartly dressed, looking very professional, and I remember thinking that her clothes didn't really match her personality, which was so bright and outgoing. That was easy to see within a few moments of meeting her.

'You must be Gina,' I said, and before I could say any more she simply said, 'Jane! Hayley has told me so much about you.'

We spent a little time talking and Hayley was right, we hit it off straight away. She asked after my children and I learned that she had been back at work for just under a year after having her first son Lewis, who was almost two years old. We chatted for a while and agreed we should meet up sometime for a night out with Hayley.

The next day I was pleasantly surprised to find an email from Gina in my inbox. 'Do you fancy getting together with Hayley and me for lunch one day?' she asked.

I didn't hesitate in replying. 'Definitely!'

A few days later I emailed Hayley and Gina and arranged a date to meet at the work canteen. The self-service restaurant was noisy and heaving with people when I walked in so I scanned around the faces looking for the girls. Gina was easy to spot – or rather her smile was. She really stood out from the crowd. I walked over to the table and she explained that something had come up and Hayley couldn't make it. But it didn't matter a jot. We chose our food and sat back down and the conversation flowed easily for the next hour. We had a blast and during lunch we discovered that we had a lot in common. Crucially, we shared a similar sense of humour and I thoroughly enjoyed her company.

After that I would often meet Gina for lunch, sometimes with other people, but sometimes just the two of us. I felt totally comfortable in her company. She was funny, honest, warm, compassionate, considerate and so kind. I was thrilled to have found such a lovely new friend.

Sometime later I was speaking to Hayley and she explained discreetly that Gina and her husband Shaun had decided to separate for a while. She told me that Gina was feeling a bit overwhelmed and wondered if I would be able to speak to her, so we could talk through the practical aspects of being a single mum. 'Of course I will,' I replied, slightly surprised. 'Why didn't she just ask me herself?'

'She didn't want to impose or put you under any pressure,' explained Hayley.

Rather than ring Gina I sent an email, saying that Hayley had told me about the separation and that if she needed anything she simply had to ask. I received a reply almost immediately, thanking me and asking if we could get together, so we agreed to meet the following day. Over lunch we talked about how I managed on my own, juggling kids and work, the practical problems, the financial help available and so on. As I left her I gave her a warm hug, saying, 'You know where I am if you need anything.'

A few days later, I happened to be throwing an Ann Summers party with a few of my girlfriends. It wasn't anything too rowdy, just an excuse for a bit of a giggle with some nibbles and a few bottles of wine. Hayley had already said she was coming. I decided to invite Gina along too. I wasn't sure if she would accept, as she would only know me and Hayley. While I thought she might appreciate the chance to let her hair down, I knew from experience it was a fragile time and she might not be ready to face a room full of strangers. When I mentioned it, though, she jumped at the chance – anything for a laugh.

The only problem was that Gina lived half an hour's drive from my house, which meant that she wouldn't be able help us out with the wine. So I told her she was welcome to stay the night.

'There are a few others staying,' I joked. 'So the first to get the beds are the lucky ones and the rest will have to crash on the floor.'

I was a bit concerned that Gina would feel out of place, but I certainly didn't need to worry. She fitted in straight away, giggling and joking with all the guests as if she'd met them all before. A couple of friends remarked on what a great laugh she was and how much they enjoyed her company. Luckily, Gina seemed to be enjoying herself immensely and I was pleased.

At the end of the night, it transpired that Gina was the only one who needed a bed for the night, but that wasn't a problem. As we waved off the last of my friends, Gina helped to tidy up, chatting away about nothing in particular, then we both flopped into an armchair each, our glasses topped up with wine, tucking into leftover nibbles just for the sake of it, and sat talking until the early hours of the morning. Gina asked about my family, about Marco and Millie, past relationships and so on. She was so easy to talk to and I felt so at ease around her that I was happy to talk about everything, even the more miserable parts of my life, and I told her all about my family.

• • •

My parents had me later on in life, so there was a big gap between my brothers and sister, and me. When I came along my sister Ann was already 21, married and pregnant. In fact my niece, Sam, was born just twenty-two days after me! My brothers, Mick and Rich, were 15 and 14 when I was born and throughout my life have been the archetypal big brothers: always overprotective, but always close.

We were a tight-knit bunch and I was brought up being told that family is everything. That meant the extended family too. I have such fond memories of my childhood. Holidays always included aunts, uncles, cousins and family friends staying together at a caravan park for the 'July Fortnight', playing on the beach together, running through the sand dunes and paddling in the sea.

Because Ann was so much older than me, and living away from home, I often forgot she was my sister. But we saw a lot of her and Sam was like a sister to me, so much so that I used to tell people she was. We shared everything and, until we were about 14, she came on every holiday with us.

As I got older, and understood the family dynamic a bit better, I was so proud to have a big sister as well as two wonderful big brothers. We were all very close and there was nothing that I couldn't share with them about my life, both positive and negative.

At the age of 16, I was already working as a dental nurse. One day in November I met Sam for lunch in town near to the practice that I worked at. She was staying with my mum, dad and me for the weekend so we made our plans for that night and I went back to work having arranged to meet her on the bus.

An hour or two later, my life changed forever, as I told Gina with a catch in my voice. Mick's wife arrived at my work and, when I went to greet her, puzzled at her arrival in the middle of the afternoon, she told me, as gently as possible, that my beloved dad had collapsed and died. She took me home and I remember standing outside our house, wanting to run through the front door to get to my mum but too afraid, because I could hear her crying from outside. Eventually I opened the door and went in, kneeled on the floor in front of my mum, buried my head in her lap and sobbed.

My dad had collapsed and died from a ruptured aneurysm at the age of just 64. All that evening, people were coming and going but I didn't really hear what they were saying – all I knew was that my dad had gone.

While the family made arrangements for the funeral, Mum and I stayed with Mick, who lived over the road from my sister, for a couple of days and I remember feeling utterly useless. I wasn't old enough to help in any practical sense so I just sat holding Mum's hand whenever I could.

My family had always been close but this terrible event made us even closer. My mum was absolutely heartbroken and I worried about her constantly.

Six weeks after his death, we spent Christmas together and did what we could to make it fun, particularly for my younger nieces and nephews. My mum was determined to make the best of it for their sake. 'It's what your dad would have wanted,' she would repeat over and over again.

On 30 January, the day before my 17th, I was at home, having booked a couple of days off for my birthday. In the middle of the morning, Mum asked me to go and collect my grandma's pension from the post office for her as we were having lunch with her shortly. I grumbled a bit, as any 16-year-old girl does, but left shouting back to my mum that I wouldn't be long. I was almost at the end of my street when Mum shouted from the window. I tutted loudly and headed back to our house. 'Sorry,' she said. 'I forgot to ask you to pick up some potatoes.' I turned to leave again, as she said, 'I love you, Jane.' There was nothing unusual in that; my family were open and honest and we regularly told each other 'I love you'.

'Love you too, Mum,' I replied, heading off once again down the street. By the time I returned, I could only have been gone forty minutes.

'I'm back,' I shouted. No response. I smiled to myself. Mum having her lunchtime nap then. I quietly opened the door to the lounge where my mum sat on the sofa and I walked over to gently wake her to tell her it was time to go to my grandma's. As soon as I reached her I knew something was very wrong. I ran round to our neighbours, bursting through the door without knocking.

'It's Mum,' I shouted. The neighbours came running back with me and the rest is just a blur. Somehow, someone had spoken to my brother who worked in the same village and he was soon there, as were an ambulance crew. They tried to save Mum but they were too late. She had suffered a fatal heart attack at the age of 59, just eleven weeks after Dad had died. I was now an orphan.

I really don't know how I would have got through those times without my extended family. My brothers and sister became everything to me – my guides, my confidants, my world.

In turn, Gina opened up to me about her past and present. She spoke a lot about Lewis and her former partner Shaun, and we shared some general banter about being better off without men, laughing at their shortcomings and how it was easier for us to be on our own. Somehow, though, when Gina said this sort of thing about Shaun, her defiant message didn't reach her eyes, so I guessed that it never reached her heart either.

World set to rights, we called it a night – but it was just the beginning for our friendship.

• • •

On another occasion soon afterwards, as we said our farewells after meeting up with a group of other people, Gina said quietly to me, 'Fancy coming round with the kids tomorrow?'

I was free and it beat hanging around my own house with the kids, so I readily agreed and the next day we introduced the three children to each other.

Marco, aged six, was quite a shy little boy, having not long started school, where he often got teased for his bright ginger hair. Millie, at four, was also quite timid, except when she was around her big brother. I think some of her shyness was my fault though, as she had been born prematurely and I'll

15

admit I was rather overprotective at times. With my two quiet children safely buckled into their car seats behind me, I watched them closely in the rear-view mirror as I drove over to Gina's house. I wasn't sure how they'd take to Gina's outgoing nature or to making a new friend in Lewis.

We pulled up on the drive at the front of the house that Gina was sharing with Lewis. I had explained to Marco and Millie that they were going to meet Mummy's new friend and that she had a little boy they could play with. They slowly hopped out of the car and stood behind me on the driveway, Millie burying her face behind my legs as we walked up to Gina's porch.

I knocked on the door and Gina opened it, greeting us all with her trademark smile. 'Hey, you two,' she said in a bubbly voice as she guided them through the front door. 'I've heard so much about you and Lewis can't wait to meet you.' It soon became clear that I needn't have worried about them getting on. While my two were quite shy and reserved, Lewis was like his mum and rushed into the room like a tornado.

'I've got a racing car track in my room, want to come and play?' he babbled. At just two years old, Lewis was falling over his words. I heard 'race', 'car', 'bedroom', but even I was unsure of the rest. Gina translated for us. 'He has his racing car track in his room,' she smiled warmly. 'He wants you to go and play.' Marco and Millie looked at me, unsure.

'It's okay,' I coaxed. 'You can go up if you want to,' and that's just what they did. Gina and Lewis's enthusiastic personalities obviously rubbed off on Marco and Millie, and within minutes we could hear them all chatting away excitedly. Marco soon took on the role of 'big brother' to Lewis and would organise what the kids were going to play or do. It wasn't just bossing the others about, though; he was loving and encouraging with it. I remember the first time that Marco and Lewis had a game of football and Marco kept letting Lewis score a goal by pretending to fall over and then praising him for how good he was. It was lovely to see.

With the children now firm friends, Gina and I started doing things with them on our days off, whether it was going to the park, day trips out, or just chilling at each other's houses with the kids playing contentedly while we caught up over a cuppa. Over time we discovered more and more mutual interests and we grew closer and closer. I introduced Gina to my other friends and family, and Gina likewise.

Emma was one of these. She had been a friend of Gina and Shaun for many years and I met her on one of our group girly nights. I instantly liked her and soon classed her as a friend. In turn, my friends all thought Gina was amazing, caring and funny, and were soon including her in any plans that we were making together.

We socialised together, we would stay over at each other's homes with the children and have meals together. Within about four months we saw each other every day and became pretty inseparable. My children already called her Auntie Gina and Lewis called me Auntie Jane.

Although Gina and Shaun were separated, as Lewis's father he was still part of Gina's life. The first time that I saw him he was working as a bouncer at one of the pubs that Gina and I often went to. As we walked to the pub, she told me that Shaun would be working and she pointed him out as we approached, but in all honesty I didn't take much notice. Having had one too many drinks I was more interested in getting into the warm with a glass of something in my hand.

The first time I met Shaun properly was at Halloween. Whenever there was an occasion, Gina would throw herself into it. Halloween was no exception and that year we decided to throw a party together. It was originally just going to be us and the kids, but she soon changed her mind about that. She invited other friends with children, and some without. Marco and Millie were also allowed to bring friends along. And all the guests were in fancy dress! Gina decorated the house and organised the games and everyone joined in – they didn't really have a choice. The apple bobbing was hilarious and even the adults had a go at it.

The party wasn't the best setting for the first meeting between Shaun and me. Shaun had promised Lewis he would come over to see him in his costume but he was late and Gina was annoyed, as was I on her behalf. When Shaun did arrive, Gina introduced us briefly. He was a big bloke, solid rather than fat, but I found him a bit stand-offish and I was a little intimidated by him. Part of me was wary of him – after all, he was Gina's ex and I couldn't help feeling protective of both her and Lewis. I said a quick hello and made my excuses to leave them alone in the kitchen, having no doubt that Gina would be waiting to give him a telling-off.

As I walked out, I spotted Lewis, who asked, 'Where's Mummy?'

'In the kitchen with Daddy,' I told him.

I wasn't quite prepared for his reaction. The look of joy on that little boy's face was one that I'll remember forever. No matter what had happened, his daddy meant everything to him.

It was my first glimpse of seeing Shaun through his son's eyes. Perhaps he wasn't all bad.

• • •

Now that Halloween was over and winter beginning to bite, my thoughts turned to Christmas shopping.

Christmas time with Gina as my friend really was magical. We both loved the build-up and I think we were more excited than the kids. We booked a day off work to scour the town centre for the perfect gifts and spent a couple of child-free evenings together with a bottle of wine, a Christmas CD and lots of wrapping paper. On Christmas morning, by 5.30, we were already on the phone to each other and we had regular telephone updates throughout the day. As it happened, that Boxing Day we were both going to be without the kids and Gina already had her day planned with her friends. 'Why don't you come along?' she asked.

'I don't really know many of them,' I replied. 'I wouldn't want to intrude.'

She told me off for being silly and said, 'That's it then. It's arranged.'

'Do I have a choice?' I laughed.

'No,' was all I got back.

So the following morning I met Gina at her house, we got ready together, then we met up with other people in town throughout the day. Everyone was very friendly and I instantly felt at ease. I had a great time and it certainly beat being sat on my own at home watching the TV.

By the end of that first year, Gina and I were inseparable. I felt lucky to have her as a friend. She was one of those people who lit up a room – loving, loud, caring, compassionate, considerate. At the same time, if she didn't agree with something, she would tell you straight away and then that would be it – she had said her piece and then the subject was dropped.

A little while after our friendship was cemented, I started dating a guy. As guys are sometimes wont to do, he was blowing a bit hot and cold on me, and I would bend Gina's ear about it every time he let me down. But Gina, as usual, didn't hesitate in pointing out the facts.

'He only wants you when it suits him,' she scolded, and though she was being blunt, her eyes looked carefully for my reaction. She squeezed my hand. 'You deserve so much better!'

At the time I thought she was quite harsh – but it soon turned out that she was right, of course. She only ever had my best interests at heart.

Gina was honest, kind and beautiful. I honestly can't think of a bad thing to say about her.

Over the years we had some wonderful times together, laughed together, cried together, my beautiful best friend. My sister of choice.

• • •

Both Gina and I suffered from frequent tonsillitis. Unfortunately, so did Lewis. When, in 2002, I booked in to have my tonsils out on a Monday, I couldn't believe it when I learned that Lewis was to come in the following day to have the same operation. I wasn't well and had to stay in overnight, and he was in the room next to me. Poor Gina was running backwards and forwards between the two rooms fussing over both of us. Shaun came to visit Lewis and I watched as he and Gina both warmly cared for their son. They made a good team and Lewis made a quick recovery. I, on the other hand, felt awful and was in a lot of pain for a couple of weeks, but Gina was there helping out despite everything she had going on with Lewis, cooking meals for us, just being an amazing friend.

Soon after we had both recovered from the op, at about 9.30 on a freezing cold Wednesday night,

I was just thinking about going to bed because I couldn't get warm, when the phone rang. I didn't answer it but it rang again straight away. I smiled to myself because I knew it was Gina – she could be very persistent when she wanted to. I picked up with a cheery 'Hey you'.

'We are going on holiday,' was all I got back.

'Okay,' I said. 'Where's this come from?'

'It's freezing and miserable, so we need a break and some sunshine,' she replied.

I couldn't argue with that!

'Sounds like a plan. Where and when you thinking?' I asked.

'Hayley's mum and dad's apartment, 22nd of May,' she answered firmly – and specifically. I was a bit flabbergasted but excited all the same. 'You have it all planned then,' I laughed. It turned out that Gina had already spoken to Hayley's parents and their apartment was empty that week, and she had jumped online to find the flights.

'Well?' she asked impatiently. 'Shall we do it?'

She didn't need to ask twice. 'Yes!' I said excitedly.

We met up the next day and got on the computer to book the flights and the car hire, and that was it. Let the countdown begin – and it really did. Every day, when I logged on to my computer at work there was an email… '24 days'… '23 days', then, finally, 'TOMORROW!!!!'

The kids were all as excited as Gina and me as we headed off to the airport. The kids chatted happily on the plane and Gina and I were like a couple of schoolgirls, giggling and chatting. We landed safely, collected our baggage and headed off to pick up our hire car. We had agreed that I would do the driving and Gina would navigate. What a big mistake that was! We had been in the car about an hour longer than we needed to be before Gina realised we had gone about 80 miles in the wrong direction. Hayley's parents had drawn a map for us and Gina had had it upside down. You might have expected us to get a bit niggly with each other, but no. We just burst out laughing, so much so that I had to pull over for a minute as I couldn't see where I was driving because of the tears running down my face.

I have so many magical memories of that holiday. My good friend Hazel had moved out to Spain the year before with her family and we managed to meet up with them for a day on the beach, which was a wonderful day out. On another afternoon, the kids were playing happily in the sand when Gina let out a deafening screech. I looked up to see her pointing at a bird that had just plucked a squid from the sea.

As it flew towards us it dropped the squid, which missed Lewis's head by an inch, then hit the floor with a thud. Lewis turned and saw the squid on the sand and screamed his head off. It was pretty grim at the time but we soon all saw the funny side of it.

One day we decided to venture out in the car to Benidorm, which was only a few miles away. The sun was red hot so I went out to the car and started the engine to allow the air conditioning to kick in while Gina rounded up the kids and made sure they were ready to go. They piled into the car chatting and giggling away with each other. We made sure all seatbelts were on and I teased Gina, 'Don't even think about navigating. After last time, I'll follow the road signs and take my chances.'

There was a quiet road that led from the apartment block to the main road and we started heading down it. I became aware of a car coming in the opposite direction on my side of the road, so I slowed down and waited for him to move over but he didn't. I started commenting on the driver, 'What's he playing at? He needs to pull over,' I grouched as I flashed my headlights. Gina was laughing but I didn't find it funny. He now had his hand out of the window shaking his fist, at which point I put my window down and held my hand up as though to say, 'What are you doing?' He started to shout at me in Spanish saying who knows what. I started to say something back. Gina was in stitches, but between gasps of air she managed to blurt out, 'It's us on the wrong side of the road! We're in Spain remember?' Realisation hit. I was horrified. I put my hand up in apology and moved over to the right side of the road. Gina couldn't contain herself, she was hysterical. In the end I couldn't help but laugh along, because Gina's incontrollable giggle was so infectious. Just like her warmth.

One of my favourite memories of the holiday is *Shrek*. Yes, the film. The three children were addicted to it, so every evening, once we had eaten and showered, the kids sat down to watch it while Gina and I had a bottle of wine and a good gossip. The best bit was at the end, though, as soon as the credits started to go up and the 'karaoke party' starts with the Sir Mix-a-Lot song 'Baby Got Back': that track that has the line about liking 'big butts'. Gina and I would already be laughing. We'd jump up onto our feet and, with the kids, dance around the room sticking our bums in the air. It was a silly thing but it sticks in my mind clear as day and as soon as I think of it, even now, I can't help but smile.

The apartment came with a pool, which was shared with a handful of other families but was very quiet. Marco, now eight, could swim, whereas six-year-old Millie and three-year-old Lewis couldn't. As soon as we arrived, Gina and I set very firm ground rules: none of them were to enter the pool without asking first, and Millie and Lewis could only go in with their armbands on, and only when at least one of us was around to keep an eye on them. The kids accepted that and would run happily around the surrounding area when they couldn't go in.

On one occasion, Gina and I were lounging in the sun while the kids played with a plastic golf set on the grass nearby. I closed my eyes for a second, feeling the warm sun on my face. Bliss. I could hear the giggles of the children and smiled to myself; it was such a lovely sound. The crickets chirped in the sunshine and I may have dozed a little, happily letting my thoughts wander lazily wherever they pleased.

All of a sudden, I heard a splash and a scream from Gina. I leaped instantly to my feet and pure instinct told me to run. I reached the pool in seconds, being only a few feet away, and I jumped straight in, oblivious to the shock of the cold water. In a flash I grabbed Lewis, who was flailing desperately in the water, pulled him to the side and lifted him up and out.

By now Gina was at the edge of the pool and I passed him up to her. They were both frightened and in tears, and Marco and Millie looked on open-mouthed. I reassured Lewis and Gina and, after a little rest, he bounded off to play golf again. It turned out that Lewis had hit the ball the wrong way and had heard it plop into the water. He had simply gone to look over the side to see where his ball was – but had leaned too far and toppled in.

'How did you get there so quick?' said Gina, who was still shaken. 'I just panicked and froze to the spot.'

'I don't know,' I answered. 'It was instinct.'

'That's why we love you,' she said. 'You are our guardian angel.'

I will never forget those words.

CHAPTER 2

REUNITED

After that initial meeting at Halloween, I met Shaun a number of times – either when he was working the doors at the bar we went to, or collecting and returning Lewis from a visit. It soon became apparent that he was very different to Gina. He may have looked big and bolshie, but he was far more reserved than her and a lot more private. In the beginning I found him hard work and I thought that he was quite rude, so I voiced this to Gina – but only the once. Even though they were not together, she told me off for saying it.

One thing that was obvious was Shaun's love for Lewis; he was a great dad and Lewis idolised him. I'm not sure Gina even realised that she was doing it, but she talked about Shaun with such love and warmth, often saying he had made her very happy and that he had made her the person she was today. Yes, she moaned and groaned about him at times, but there was never much conviction in this – and I could see he felt the same about her.

In spite of their living apart, it was blindingly obvious to me that Gina and Shaun still loved each other deeply, so I was genuinely thrilled when they decided they were getting back together. It was 2003, Lewis was now four and it was brilliant for him to see his parents happy together again. And Gina couldn't wipe the smile off her face, bless her.

The kids and I still saw Gina and Lewis just as much as we always had. The only difference now was that, at times, Shaun was there as well. He really was great with the kids. Millie took a real shine to him and loved it when he showed her any attention. Both Marco and Millie warmed to him as quickly as they had Gina and were soon calling him Uncle Shaun. While I was pleased for my friend that she was happy, I still found Shaun a bit tricky – but all that was about to change.

After my divorce, I had bought a house that needed a lot of work. I was proud of the progress I had made and my brothers helped out whenever they could, but there always seemed to be something that still needed to be done. I was quite taken aback when, a couple of months after they got back together, Gina boldly suggested that Shaun could give me a helping hand with some of the DIY I was struggling with. I felt it was an imposition and that Shaun wouldn't want to help, but he quietly went along with Gina's plan – as usual. Marco and Millie, his biggest fans, couldn't wait for Shaun to see their house.

The following day, Gina, Shaun and Lewis arrived at my house as promised.

'Hope that kettle's on!' said a loud voice as they let themselves in the back door. 'I'm on strike till I've had a cuppa.'

It was the sort of comment I expected from my brothers – but this time it was Shaun. I was stunned. I think that was the most Shaun had ever said to me!

For whatever reason, Shaun appeared more relaxed that day. He wasn't chatting away ten to the dozen, that wasn't his style, but he genuinely seemed to make more of an effort and I started to warm to him. I slowly learned that he was a bit of a gentle giant – and not the obnoxious, intimidating person I had initially perceived him to be. I couldn't help but notice how much pride was in his voice whenever Lewis came into the conversation, and that gave him Brownie points with me.

The next time I saw Gina, I couldn't help but comment that I'd thought Shaun had disliked me until that day.

'You're daft,' she reassured me. 'Don't worry; Shaun is like that with everyone to start with. Believe it or not he is quite shy. It takes a long time for the real Shaun to come out.' Then she added, with a chuckle, 'You're lucky – it's only been a few months. Sometimes it can take years.'

From that day on, I began to discover that Shaun wasn't the intimidating, stand-offish man I had believed him to be at first. He was obviously a very private man and, on reflection, my being so guarded with him initially must have made things more awkward. Over the next few months I built up a really good friendship with Shaun. Gina was generally thrilled that we got along so well. As for me, all I knew was that my best friend was so happy – and that was good enough for me!

• • •

Lewis had always been a 'sickly' child, constantly having a cough and cold, tonsillitis or a chest infection. Early in 2003 he was unwell again and, at first, we thought it was nothing unusual. He had been given some standard antibiotics by the doctor.

But they weren't working – and Gina couldn't get his temperature down, no matter what she did. She called me to say she was taking him to the walk-in centre as it was out of hours for the doctor's surgery and I wished her luck with the appointment.

When she phoned me a short while later, I could immediately hear the concern in her voice.

'We have to take him to the hospital!' she told me tearfully. 'They think he could have pneumonia.'

I did my best to reassure her and promised her I would be at the hospital as soon as I could. I arrived not long after Gina and Shaun, who confirmed that Lewis did indeed have pneumonia and that it was so bad that they were taking him straight to theatre to try to clear his lungs out. They were both distraught. We paced the waiting room with Gina's mum and dad anxiously waiting for news. After what felt like a lifetime, he was brought back to the ward, wired up to machines, with drips in both his hands and his face covered in a mask from the ventilator, which was helping him to breathe. He looked so tiny lying there, too small to be fighting such a serious illness. My children were with their dad so I was free to offer any support that I could.

I didn't want to leave. I needed to be there for my friend.

A few hours after he came back to the ward, the doctors said they were pleased with Lewis's progress so they wanted to see if he could breathe on his own. Gina was so terrified she couldn't watch as they pulled the tubes out of his throat, so Shaun sat by his son's side holding his hand while I gave a step-by-step rundown to Gina of what they were doing, standing with my arms around her to comfort her. Suddenly, I said, 'His chest is moving. He's doing it. He is breathing by himself!' Gina's body shuddered as she broke down and sobbed with relief. She had nearly lost her beautiful boy but now it seemed the worst was over.

Sometime later I left Gina and Shaun at the hospital. They promised me they would call me if there was any change at all. Over the next few days Lewis did remarkably well. He was still poorly but would sit up in bed to read a book or attempt a jigsaw. Gina, by her own admission, 'didn't do sick' so I would take over when Lewis was vomiting, or just to give Gina and Shaun a break from the bedside vigil.

At last the doctors said that all the fluid had gone from Lewis's lungs so they could take the chest drain out. They explained that this wouldn't be nice and would be painful for Lewis but it was a huge step forward. Gina looked at me and said, 'He will hate me for this.' I knew what she was saying: that he was too young to understand why his loving mum would let him go through this trauma while she was there to stop it; that he wouldn't realise that it was all for his own good. So I took Lewis's little hand in mine and said, 'Come with Auntie Jane, sweetheart. We have to go and see the special doctor.'

During the next few painful minutes, I held him tight in my arms with tears pouring down my face as he struggled against me. Then at last it was done and I cuddled him and told him how brave he was. The nurse gave him a sticker, a bravery certificate and a lollipop for being such a good boy, and he walked out of the room with a beaming smile to show them off to everybody. Gina hugged him and, amid tears of relief, she looked at me and mouthed, 'Thank you.' I smiled and said, 'It's fine.'

A couple of days later Lewis was allowed home and made a complete recovery. To this day, he vaguely remembers being in hospital and has the scars to prove it, but as yet has never asked me why I let the doctors hurt him. At least now he would be old enough to understand.

Mother's Day fell shortly after Lewis came home and, when I came down in the morning, I was surprised to see three envelopes on my kitchen table. I opened my cards from Marco and Millie, then I got to the third. Inside I found a lovely card with the words 'Like a mum to me' across the front. Gina had helped Lewis to write his name inside and there was a simple message from Gina and Shaun saying, 'Thank you for everything.'

That weekend, it was my ex-husband's turn to have Marco and Millie so Gina and Shaun insisted I joined them for a Mother's Day meal with Lewis. As usual, Gina wouldn't take no for an answer. 'Like the card says,' she insisted. 'You are like a mum to him so it's only right you come out with us for Mother's Day.' Eventually I agreed and the four of us went out for a lovely meal. It just felt like the natural thing to do.

• • •

Shaun and Gina were really happy together the second time around and in time I met a new partner. Kev and I got together that year and when I introduced him to Gina and Shaun (for approval, as Gina put it), he and Shaun hit it off straight away. 'Perfect,' thought Gina and I. We would do things together as two families.

Coincidentally, the men were both keen to learn to scuba-dive, so Gina and I encouraged them to enrol on a local course together. They both qualified and soon were going off to different places to dive, leaving Gina and I to have our girly time. Shaun was still a bouncer and worked at weekends, and Kev got a job with him some time later, which meant that Gina and I could have girly nights in most weekends. It all worked out beautifully.

We also spent a lot of time all together as two families, having barbecues, going for a drink or a meal, taking the kids on days out and celebrating birthdays, Christmases and New Year's Eves together. I come from a family that has always been into racing and Shaun was a big motorbike fan, which meant Gina became a big bike fan too. My nephews Stephen and Paul raced sidecars, and Gina and Shaun would often come along to watch them race.

In the summer of 2003, Gina and I decided to take the kids to Gulliver's Kingdom, the theme park in Matlock, for a treat. We had to go in two cars as we couldn't all fit in one and we stopped at a garage for fuel on the way, so Gina and I brought some sweets for the journey. After we set off again, I was driving along chatting with Marco and Millie, munching sweets, when all of a sudden I felt something hard in my mouth – I had pulled a filling out on a toffee eclair. 'Great,' I thought. 'If I have toothache all day this is not going to be fun!'

We pulled into a parking space and Gina opened her car door and held out her hand to me. 'I've only gone and pulled my filling out,' she said. I couldn't believe it, what were the chances of that happening to both of us?

It didn't stop the fun, of course, and we had a great day. The kids loved it, the weather was fantastic. But a week after the trip I got a letter through the post, saying I had been flashed by a speed camera both on the way to Gulliver's Kingdom and on the way back. I was mortified. I racked my brains, trying to remember if I had been following Gina or she had been following me, then I decided I would blame her anyway (in a fun way). As I went to pick up the phone to call her she rang me. She had received exactly the same letter and was ringing to try to blame me. We couldn't help laughing. Kev and Shaun were not so amused but joked that, in future, we were not to be allowed out together again unless accompanied by a responsible adult.

Christmas was always a good time. Gina and I had already established that we both loved Christmas and we spent weeks getting ready, and spending far too much money. Now Shaun started a tradition of ringing our house and asking to speak to Marco and Millie, then putting on a voice and pretending to be Father Christmas. Then Kev would return the call to Lewis. None of the kids guessed that it wasn't really Father Christmas until they were old enough to stop believing in Santa altogether.

Over Christmas, we started to think about holidays. We all spent so much time with each other that it only seemed natural we should go away together and, once it had been mentioned, there was no stopping us. When Gina was on a mission, she was like a dog with a bone and completely engrossed until her task was complete, whether it was a project at work, the weekly shop online, finding an unusual present, or booking a holiday. So when she rang me a couple of days later to say that she had worked out how much it would cost for us all to go to Disneyland Paris, I wasn't at all surprised. Better still, the dates she had chosen were only a few weeks away! That was it, decision made, we confirmed the booking and got on with the packing.

It didn't take long for the time to come around and soon we were off. I honestly can't say who was the most excited – Gina and me, or the three children. Kev and Shaun, being easy-going guys, just did what they were told and went along with it, as always. It was early 2004 and it was freezing, but that didn't stop us making the most of everything. We had an amazing time!

To people looking on, if Lewis hadn't been the double of his mum, I guess it would have been hard to tell which child belonged to which adult. We all treated the children exactly the same as if they were our own. Millie, then seven, spent most of the holiday perched up on Shaun's shoulders and Lewis, like me, wasn't keen on the bigger rides so we would go look at other things while the others went on. In the evenings we would all go out for a meal together, then when the exhausted kids fell into bed we would sit in one of our adjoining rooms, chatting and making plans until the early hours. Plans that included other days out, chill-out time together and more holidays!

As far as we were concerned, we had all the time in the world.

• • •

By mid-2004, Kev and I were really happy together and agreed, with great excitement, that we wanted to take our relationship into a new phase. He was a fantastic stepdad to Marco and Millie, and we decided it was time to add to our little brood, so we started trying for a baby. We chose to keep it quiet in case it didn't happen, but I wouldn't dream of keeping such a secret from Gina. So one day, over a cuppa in my living room, I confided, 'I'm not supposed to be telling anyone, but Kev and I are going to try for a baby. If it happens, it happens. What will be will be.'

Gina grinned immediately.

'I knew you would be excited for us,' I said.

'Not just you, us,' she replied.

I looked at her quizzically. 'You've lost me.'

'Shaun and I have decided to try for another one too,' she blurted out happily.

I shouldn't have been surprised. Gina's sister Keri had recently announced she was pregnant again, to Gina's obvious delight, and Gina had never hidden the fact that she wanted more children. We flung our arms around each other and danced around like a couple of toddlers at a birthday party. This was going to be something else that we could share.

After that, we would spend hours trying to calculate the best time to get pregnant – and comforting each other when, month after month, it didn't happen. But the frequent disappointments never stopped us planning how life would be with a new baby. We kept each other strong.

Eventually, though, it did get a little overwhelming, so it was a welcome distraction when Kev and Shaun announced they were taking us to Dublin for our birthdays, for a joint weekend break. Gina and I had birthdays a week apart; Gina's on the 24th of January, mine on the 31st. We knew that we would both miss our children but the idea of an adults only weekend was exciting. We added the Dublin dates to our diaries and started to look forward to the trip.

The excitement also put us in the holiday mood and we decided that we would all like to have a proper family holiday abroad, so Gina was on a mission again. After all her research, we decided on the Dominican Republic and booked the holiday for Easter 2005.

Before we could start our globe-trotting, though, there was Christmas. Yippee! Our favourite time of year. Gina and I went into the usual seasonal frenzy, rushing around, shopping together, making plans, but I noticed Gina seemed a bit quiet at times. Eventually, I asked her if she was okay, but she simply said she just felt a bit run-down.

'You're too excited about Santa!' I joked. Then a thought struck me. 'Or you could be pregnant?'

'I can't be,' she answered sadly. 'I've had my period.'

But I wasn't convinced. She simply wasn't herself. I persuaded her to buy a test and we sat looking at the little stick anxiously, jiggling and fidgeting with anticipation. The two minutes we had to wait seemed like an hour but finally we watched two little blue lines appear and we looked at each other with soppy grins – then burst into tears. I was so thrilled for her, even though I will admit that my joy, while genuine, was tinged with the tiniest bit of envy as I was so desperate to be in the same happy position. But, hey, if it couldn't be me, this was the next best thing!

I watched Gina get in her car, beaming from ear to ear, on her way to tell Shaun that he was going to be a dad again and let Lewis know that he was going to have a little brother or sister. She also couldn't wait to tell her sister, Keri, who was due to have her own baby in February. I knew how thrilled they all would be and knew Gina was overjoyed at the prospect of being a mum again. A happy tear rolled down my cheek as I waved her off.

• • •

On the day of our break away to Dublin, we arrived at the airport and settled ourselves into a bar to wait for our flight. As the boys got the round in, we were all teasing Gina, because she could only have a soft drink, but she really didn't care. Nothing was going to spoil this long-awaited weekend.

In Dublin, we found the accommodation we had booked and a very pleasant lady welcomed us and showed us to our room. But her friendly manner proved to be deceiving.

'Oh my God!' was all I could say when I opened the door. The room was filthy and we had twin beds, not a double as booked. I ran round to the room next door and bumped into Gina on her way out.

'I'm going to have words with someone,' she said, and off she disappeared down the stairs.

'So it wasn't just our room,' I thought.

Gina soon reappeared and explained that the lady had told her housekeeping had not done our rooms yet, as we had arrived a little earlier than expected. To give them time to rectify the situation we had a quick shower, got changed and headed out to explore. After a lovely meal, we rounded off the evening by trying out a few bars. As the night wore on, I noticed Gina was a little quiet but, when I asked, she said she was just tired. She was pregnant, and not drinking, while we were letting our hair down so I thought no more about it.

When we got back to our bed and breakfast, we were horrified to see the rooms were just as they had been before we left – disgusting! It was now the early hours of the morning and we were all exhausted so we agreed to make do for the night and flopped into bed, shattered. I refused to get between the sheets so slept fully clothed on top of the bed – as did Gina and Shaun, we discovered the following morning.

The next day, we ate breakfast and beat a hasty retreat to find somewhere a little more luxurious for our second night. Never mind the money, we weren't staying there another moment. Shaun remembered a hotel he had stayed in a couple of years previously on a rugby tour. What a difference! The place was perfect and even had a swimming pool and sauna. Naturally, Gina and I decided to take full advantage of the facilities and planned a couple of hours relaxing on our final morning while Kev and Shaun headed off to the on-site gym.

As we sat in the bar area having a coffee and waiting for the men, I asked Gina, 'Is everything okay? You don't seem yourself?'

To my alarm, a tear ran down her cheek. I put my arms around her. 'What is it, babe?'

'I'm bleeding,' she replied.

'Oh Gina, why didn't you say something?' I asked. 'Does Shaun know?'

She shook her head. 'I don't want to ruin this weekend for everyone.'

'Don't be silly,' I told her, sternly. 'Let's go and find him.'

We were due to fly home in a couple of hours and, to be honest, Gina seemed relieved to have got it off her chest. Of course, I was desperately concerned for my friend but doing my utmost not to show it. After we landed, Gina went directly to the doctor's surgery and rang me as soon as her appointment was over. I picked up, half-dreading the news I could be about to hear.

'Everything is fine,' she gushed, happily. 'The baby's heartbeat is strong and they just advised me to rest for a while.'

Relief flooded over me and I felt a weight lift from my mind. Then something else occurred to me. How was Gina being pregnant going to affect our holiday to the Caribbean?

I left Gina to get over her scare for a few days before I broached the subject.

'Oh, I'll be fine,' she said breezily.

But we decided to pop into the travel agent's to double check.

We didn't get the answer we were hoping for. The travel agent explained that Gina would be in the second trimester of her pregnancy and wouldn't be allowed to take a long-haul flight. We were absolutely devastated. The holiday we had dreamed of had gone! The travel agent went on to explain that Gina and Shaun could change their booking to a European holiday so that they didn't lose any money, but my family couldn't change our booking as we didn't have a valid reason. So that was it. There was to be no joint holiday.

We were all a bit down for a few days, but we accepted what had happened. Gina having a baby on the way was, of course, far more important than a holiday. Besides, we reasoned, there would be many more years of holidays stretching ahead of us so we could make up for it at a later date. Gina and Shaun rearranged their holiday for later in the year after the baby was born, while we continued with our plans for the Dominican Republic.

A few weeks later, I had a cold and no matter what I did I just couldn't seem to shake it off completely. The red nose and sneezing had gone, but I was still horribly lethargic. Valentine's Day came around and, after weeks of this, I still felt no better. 'I wonder…' I thought.

That day, I had a busy schedule of meetings, but I made time to pop quickly to the shop before lunch and then did the test. A grin spread across my face as those tell-tale blue lines appeared. I was pregnant! At last. I was over the moon and my first thought was, 'I've got to tell Gina!'

I had already arranged to meet Gina for lunch at 12.30 p.m. I looked at the clock. Five to twelve I would have to wait for another thirty-five minutes. I groaned inwardly, it felt like a lifetime away. At last the time came, so I headed over towards the building that Gina worked in and saw her walking towards me. By now, she had a little bump showing and, seeing that, I could barely contain my own excitement!

'Hey you,' I said, as casually as possible. 'How are you feeling?'

Gina had suffered with morning sickness but it was now thankfully starting to pass. We chatted briefly about that and then I asked if she had had any news from her sister Keri yet.

'Yes,' she said excitedly, grinning from ear to ear. 'I have a new nephew called Nathan. He was born last night.'

We chatted about the new baby, his weight, Keri's labour and so on, and I asked her to pass on my love to Keri and her family. 'So how do you feel about being an auntie again?' I asked while trying to keep a straight face.

'I can't wait to meet him...' she trailed off, then looked at me and finally clocked the beaming expression on my face. Her eyes lit up. Then she burst into tears.

'Are you saying what I think you're saying?' she asked. All I could do was nod, as my own tears threatened to spill over. She was so happy for me. After a massive bear hug, we both started talking ten to the dozen, tripping over our words.

'What do Kev, Marco and Millie think about it?' she asked. 'And why didn't you ring me as soon as you knew?'

'Because I literally just found out half an hour ago,' I replied. 'And I haven't told them yet.'

To some, it may seem odd that I chose to tell my best friend before the baby's dad or my children, but those who knew the friendship that Gina and I shared would understand completely. The conversation did not stray away from babies all lunchtime, which was fine by both of us, and as we said our goodbyes it dawned on me that I would now have to wait a few more hours to tell my family the good news.

I was so looking forward to telling Kev that he was going to be a dad. I spent all afternoon planning what I would say and do to make it really special.

On the way home, I bought an ornament of a small family – a man, woman and baby. As I waited for him to come home from work, the hands on the clock seemed to stand still. Finally, I heard his key in the door and, as he walked in, I handed him his gift.

'What's this for?' he asked, confused.

'So you never forget,' I replied.

'Forget what?' he asked.

'The day that I told you that you were going to be a dad,' I said, trying to keep my emotions in check.

Kev grinned and pulled me to him. 'So you're pregnant?' he whispered in my ear. I nodded, choked with happiness.

Marco and Millie were so excited when I broke the news to them, after telling Kev. The first thing Millie wanted to do was to ring Auntie Gina and tell her she was going to have a new brother or sister, so I didn't let on that she already knew.

Gina and I already shared most things, and to top it off we were pregnant together, which meant that our children would be born close and hopefully grow up together.

Life couldn't be more perfect.

CHAPTER 3

BOUNCING BABIES

The summer of 2005, when both Gina and I were heavily pregnant, was red hot. One scorching afternoon, the kids and I were round at Gina's while the men were at work. They had plans to join us for a barbecue later. Gina had been to buy some big bags of ice cubes to keep the drinks cold and we sat in the garden, trying to stay in the shade while the kids played in the paddling pool.

Suddenly Gina said, 'I've had enough of this.'

'What?' I said.

'We can't drink anyway,' she said.

'What do you mean?' I asked.

She didn't reply. She just stood up, went into the house and came out with two washing up bowls full of ice cubes and told me to put my feet in. Laughing, I plunged them in and it was bliss. We were instantly cool but, naturally, the ice cubes melted and she had no more left in the freezer for the drinks, but we were frazzled and past caring.

After a while, we started to get ready for the barbecue and tidy up a bit, and Gina poured what was left of the ice cubes that had been cooling our feet into a bucket and then put Shaun and Kev's beer in it to keep it cold.

'Let's keep it between us,' she giggled. 'Don't tell the boys.'

That was typical of Gina. She was mischievous. Mischievous in a lovely way.

Gina's baby was due in August and mine in October, so we prepared for the imminent arrivals together, shopping for essentials like clothes, nappies, toiletries. We even packed our hospital suitcases together and we spent hours trawling through books of baby names, joking about the really old-fashioned names, trying out various suggestions with our respective surnames – and laughing at some of the results. We would string names together that all started with the same letter. For example, Harold Howard Hibberd or Rupert Ronald Richardson. Gina nicknamed my growing bump Zebedee, after the character in the children's programme *The Magic Roundabout* because the baby was constantly moving around.

As our due dates approached, the midwife became a little concerned that Gina's baby may have been breech, so the hospital organised an extra ultrasound for her quite late on in her pregnancy. But Shaun couldn't get the time off work to accompany her. So Gina asked me to go with her – and it was such an honour. You could easily make out the shape of a little baby, arms and legs moving as much as they could in the little space that was left. The baby didn't seem too happy at being prodded and you could see him squirming as the nurse ran the transducer over Gina's tummy. But I remember how bright Gina's eyes were as she looked at the blurry but beautiful image wriggling around on the screen in front of her. It's something I will never forget.

On the morning of 27 July 2005, shortly after five in the morning, my phone beeped, alerting me to a text. I sat up with a start. Why would anyone be texting at this time of the morning? I panicked, thinking something must be wrong... but no. It was quite the opposite.

'My waters have broken, here we go,' Gina had texted.

I felt my heart jump with excitement and I quickly texted back, 'Are you getting contractions yet?'

'No,' she replied. 'We'll be over to yours soon.'

We had arranged that when Gina and Shaun needed to go to the hospital, I would have Lewis at my house for as long as necessary. She didn't wait long to come over, either. At 7.10 a.m., there was a knock on the door. I opened it to see Gina's big beaming smile, with Shaun standing calmly by her side.

'Get the kettle on then,' she said. By now Gina was getting just very mild contractions about every twenty minutes.

'Is it okay if I just stay here till we have to get to the hospital?' she asked.

'Don't be silly,' I scolded. 'I can't think of anywhere else I would want you to be, you don't need to ask!!'

I will confess a part of me was jealous she was in labour – because I couldn't wait for it to be my turn. My ever-growing bump was making me tired and, if I'm honest, a bit grouchy at times. I had taken early maternity leave as Millie had been born prematurely and the consultant didn't want to risk the chance of the new baby being born too early as well, so I was playing a long and boring waiting game.

We sat chatting in the living room together and it was obvious that Gina's labour was progressing, albeit slowly. Hours passed and still not much was happening.

'I've got an idea,' I said, and walked out of the room with a curious Gina watching me. When I returned, she burst out laughing. I had brought in a big rubber gym ball, the kind you use for doing exercises on.

'Bounce on this,' I said. 'It might help speed things up.'

One of our favourite activities of late had been to watch programmes on midwives and babies in anticipation of giving birth ourselves and this was one of the things we had seen. She did as she was told and I sat on the floor in front of her while she gently bounced up and down. It didn't take long for the contractions to become stronger and more regular and, as she was in pain, I helped Gina set up the TENS machine that she had hired.

After an hour Gina was starting to struggle. Shaun wasn't confident talking to strangers on the phone, and he knew they would want to speak to Gina, so I rang the number from the hospital paperwork for him and explained the situation as he paced up and down constantly, not quite sure what to do. He was so racked with anxiety that I'm not convinced he could have sat still long enough to hold a conversation with the midwife. After I told them what was happening, they spoke to Gina and advised that it was time for her to go in, so we packed up the car and I dropped them off at the hospital. Lewis stayed in the car so he could come home with me. As I drove away I turned to see Gina's head buried in Shaun's shoulder as she waited for another contraction to pass before they made their way inside.

'Next time you see Mummy and Daddy, you will have a new baby brother or sister,' I told Lewis, excitedly. Unfazed, he calmly asked what I was cooking for his tea.

Back home I made dinner for Lewis, Marco and Millie, tucked them all up in bed, put on a DVD for them to watch in the bedroom and kissed them goodnight. I kept anxiously looking at my phone to check I hadn't missed any calls. Just after 7 p.m. the call came.

'It's a boy,' gushed a delighted Shaun. 'They are both doing just fine. We've decided to go with the name Ashton.'

They had chosen Ashton from a baby book and given him the middle name of Jack, after Gina's granddad. Gina had said she could shorten it to AJ if they wanted, and she liked that.

'He can't wait to meet you all,' Shaun continued.

I couldn't wait either. I asked Shaun to give Gina and Ashton a kiss from me and told him to keep me updated. Three hours later the phone rang again.

'We can come home,' said Shaun, delighted.

We arranged that Kev would go and collect them from the hospital and I would take all the children over to Gina and Shaun's house in Loughborough to meet them there. I went to wake them up and tell them the good news. Marco, who had been wide awake when Shaun rang the first time, had been so excited he hadn't slept. He jumped out of bed and quickly dressed himself. Millie and Lewis were a different matter. I gently coaxed them out of a deep sleep and helped them to put dressing gowns over their pyjamas and slip their feet into slippers. They both looked pretty disgruntled at being woken up and didn't appear to understand what all the fuss was about, but I managed to load them into the car and we were on our way.

I was as excited as a kid at Christmas. I couldn't wait to meet Ashton and have a long cuddle, even if his sleepy sibling seemed unconcerned at his arrival. For a while the two little ones were quiet, half-slumbering in the back seat of the car. But halfway to the house, Lewis seemed to come to his senses and he suddenly exclaimed, 'Auntie Jane, have I really got a new baby brother?'

'You sure have, sweetheart,' I said. 'And I bet he can't wait to meet his big brother.'

'I'm going to be the bestest big brother ever,' he replied.

I couldn't help but smile.

We arrived at Gina and Shaun's about ten minutes before they did. I closed the curtains and put the lamp on to make sure that everywhere was nice and cosy, and the children sat sleepily on the sofa. But they soon woke up when the beautiful new baby was carried into the living room in his car seat, wrapped in a soft white blanket. He was perfect. He was the double of his brother – in fact he looked like Lewis had been put in the tumble dryer and shrunk to baby size again.

Lewis was thrilled to meet his tiny sibling. Shaun placed him gently into Lewis's little arms and Lewis kissed him attentively on top of his head while Marco and Millie fussed over him. He was dressed in a simple white Babygro with a little hat on, and as I gently pulled the hat off, I noticed that he had lovely dark hair – just like his mummy and daddy. I went and put my arms around Gina, who was shattered but thrilled, and we were soon both in tears as we looked at all the children together. Shaun was grinning like a Cheshire cat.

'I'm so proud of you both. Congratulations,' was all I could manage to say. Then it was time for cuddles with the gorgeous little Ashton.

Obviously, having a new baby and a six year old to look after, Gina was busy in the weeks that followed – but that didn't stop us spending just as much time together. Sometimes, she would put her hand on my bump and say, 'Hurry up, baby. Auntie Gina wants to meet you and Ashton wants a playmate.'

Eventually, on 19 October, I started getting 'niggles' and I couldn't wait to ring Gina and tell her. New baby or not she was at my house within an hour. We spent a couple of hours together as my labour progressed until she had to go and get her boys bathed and in bed, and my brother Mick arrived to babysit my two for the night.

At last, in the late evening, it was time to go to the hospital. I remember Kev teasing me at 3.45 a.m., 'If you hurry up I can ring Shaun before he goes to work!' Shaun was working as a lorry driver back then and would leave home at 4.15 a.m. most days. At the time, racked as I was by labour pains, I really did not see the funny side. Nonetheless, our beautiful little girl, Anni-Mae, obliged – arriving at 4.10 a.m. Kev's mum was present for the birth but, apart from her, Shaun and Gina were the first people to hear the news. I still remember talking to Gina on the phone before they had even finished sorting me out and her voice was so bubbly and full of excitement for us.

Like Gina, I was told a couple of hours later that I could go home. Marco had still been up when I went into hospital the night before, so he knew the baby was definitely coming, but we hadn't told him that Anni-Mae had arrived. As we got out of the car on the driveway, he ran to the door and opened it, saw her little pink hat and grinned broadly.

'I've got another little sister,' he exclaimed. Then he looked at her face and laughed. 'She's all wrinkly, Mum.'

He was right: she had a very cross expression on her face. But one of the things I had noticed as soon as she had been born was her lovely, deep red full lips which, luckily, she still has now. Wrinkly or not, she was absolutely beautiful.

Millie, who had been asleep through the whole happy drama, was still in bed. By the time she got up, Marco had Anni-Mae cradled in his arms. She walked into the lounge, rubbing sleep from her eyes.

She looked at Marco, then at me and my smaller tummy, then back at Marco, then promptly burst into tears. She was overwhelmed by excitement.

'This is your little sister, Anni-Mae,' I said gently.

Once she'd got over the shock, Millie was all smiles and couldn't wait to hold her baby sister. She soon had Anni-Mae in her arms – nervously at first, like she was afraid the baby would break, but once Anni-Mae opened her mouth and bawled loudly to inform us she was hungry, she realised that if the baby wasn't comfortable, she would definitely let us know.

With Anni-Mae on their laps, Marco and Millie posed for endless photographs, which was unusual as neither of them liked having their pictures taken. They were even a little miffed when Mick asked if he could have a cuddle because neither of them wanted to put her down.

Gina arrived at my house just after 9 a.m. – and she couldn't wait to get through the door! She handed Ashton to me and scooped Anni-Mae up in her arms. 'Hello, princess,' she said, smothering her with kisses. 'I'm your Auntie Gina.'

Princess was a name that Shaun used for one of his own nieces, Chelsea, and Gina used for her niece, Rebecca. It confirmed what I already knew:

to them we were family. After that, 'princess' stuck, and both Shaun and Gina always referred to Anni-Mae that way. All cards and present tags would read 'To our little princess, Anni-Mae'.

From that moment on, our two families merged and grew together. It was great being able to talk to Gina about sleepless nights, teething, milestones the children were reaching and all the things that matter to parents. We never did run out of things to talk about. It really was just like one big happy family.

In early 2006, we decided to make that family connection official. Kev and I opted to have Anni-Mae christened and there was never any doubt who we wanted as her godparents. We knew Gina and Shaun wouldn't object but we arranged a rare night out, just the four of us, so that we could ask them formally anyway. They agreed instantly and were really honoured to have been asked. We also asked Kev's brother Andy and their auntie Sue, as well as my nephew Stephen.

Gina was a great support, helping me prepare for the day. She designed the invitations on the computer and printed them out for me, helped me choose Anni-Mae's christening gown and went through the arrangements for the day with me. Shortly before the christening, she said she wanted to get Anni-Mae something really different for a gift.

'You don't need to get her anything,' I told her. 'Having you as her auntie and godmother is the best present she could have!' I knew it fell on deaf ears, though.

Anni-Mae was christened on 16 April 2006, which was Easter Sunday, at the age of six months. She looked so angelic in her long silk cream christening gown and smiled on cue for all the guests. Gina had a huge grin plastered across her face all day, especially when she stood at the front of the church to repeat her vows as a godparent after the vicar. Anni-Mae was very well behaved but she did start to get a bit grumpy towards the end, just when we wanted to take photos. But as soon as she was in Gina's arms she was smiling again.

Gina and Shaun did not have Lewis and Ashton officially christened, but if anyone asked who I was she always said 'The boys' godmother' or 'The boys' auntie'.

Later in the day, it was time for Anni-Mae to receive her gifts. Gina had meant what she said about the unusual present. Their gift was wrapped in pretty pink paper with ribbons and bows, and 'LADY Anni-Mae' written on the tag. As I opened it and saw the contents, I was thrilled. It was so unusual and had obviously been thought about a lot. They had bought her a little piece of Scotland, literally. Anni-Mae has a lovely certificate that states she is a 'Lady' and that she can officially use the noble title if she wishes.

'It just makes it official that she is a princess,' explained Gina. They also gave her a lovely bracelet and a delicate little cross charm, and from that day forward, for all Anni-Mae's birthdays and at Christmas, Gina and Shaun would buy another charm as one of her presents. At Christmas, she got a little silver present, at Easter a tiny silver egg, and on her first birthday a miniature pair of shoes, as she was just starting to walk. There was always so much thought behind each and every one.

Anni-Mae has seen the bracelet and she knows how special it is, but I am keeping it safely tucked away until her 18th birthday. It would break my heart if anything happened to it.

• • •

Nine months after the christening, I had to go into hospital for a minor procedure. I had not been well since I'd had Anni-Mae and suffered with a lot of 'ladies' problems', which caused stomach pains and anaemia, and left me feeling tired and run-down.

Gina was constantly nagging at me, 'Go to the doctors! I'll take you.' In fact, she eventually phoned the surgery to make the appointment for me and said, 'Right you're going to the doctor's on Thursday at two.'

To be honest, I was relieved when the gynaecologist offered to perform a minor procedure, which had a good chance of solving my problems. I was booked in for 7 February 2007 and the day before, as we parted company, Gina wished me luck and told me to ring her as soon as I was home. The operation was a routine and simple one and although I had been informed – as with any operation – that there were risks, the expectation was that I would be out around lunchtime, as I would only be under anaesthetic for around twenty minutes.

I arrived at the hospital around 7.30 a.m. and was being wheeled to theatre by eight o'clock – one of the perks of having private health insurance through my job. Gina texted me while I was on the way to the hospital to say she was thinking about me and I replied light-heartedly, 'I'll be fine, speak to you soon.'

But it turned out that wasn't the case at all. I vaguely remember waking up in recovery and noticing the clock on the wall said 4.10 p.m. 'The clock has stopped,' I said gruffly to the nurse.

'It's all right, it's all right,' soothed the nurse. 'Don't worry about that. Go back to sleep.'

But I looked again and said, 'Your clock is broken though.'

I tried so hard to keep my eyes open and I was in far more pain than I had expected, but I must have drifted back to sleep as the next time I opened my eyes I was back in my room on the ward. Everything seemed hazy and almost in slow motion. I was aware of Kev by my side and the intense pain I was in, but I was only semi-conscious.

Suddenly Gina was at the foot of my bed. I honestly don't know if she had just arrived or if she had been in the room all along. She put her hand on my foot and, sobbing, said, 'What have they done to you?'

I was frightened. What did she mean? Why was I in so much pain? She sat down on the other side of the bed to Kev and gently took my hand. I was aware of tears coursing down my cheeks but I wasn't really sure why I was crying. Then Kev said, 'We need to tell you something. Things didn't go as planned in theatre and they had to do an emergency hysterectomy.'

I felt crushed. Now I knew why there were so many machines, and fluid and blood drips. It explained the pain and the grogginess. I later learned that the clock in recovery hadn't broken: I had been in theatre all day.

I find it hard to describe the loss I felt when I learned of the hysterectomy. Yes, I already had three wonderful children, but I was only 34 – and the decision as to whether or not my family was complete had been taken away from me. I was devastated. But there was more to come.

Sometime later, I don't know whether it was minutes or hours, I was still struggling with the pain and Gina rang the bell for the nurse. The nurse took my hand and told me she would be back shortly with some painkillers, then she turned to Kev and Gina and asked in a hushed voice, 'Have you told her?'

'Yes,' they replied, together.

'What, everything?' she asked, and they slowly shook their heads.

'You need to tell her soon, before she finds out for herself,' she said sadly, then she quietly left the room leaving us alone.

'What, what is it?' I asked.

Kev looked at his feet, Gina's tears began to flow again.

'Am I going to die?' was all I could say. I really thought that was what they needed to tell me, either that or that they had found some sort of tumour when they opened me up in theatre.

Both Kev and Gina responded immediately, 'Of course not, don't be silly.'

'Then what?' I asked between tears. As gently as they could, they explained that during the panic in theatre my bowel had been damaged and part of it had been removed. As I tried to comprehend what they were telling me, Kev quietly told me that I now had a colostomy bag. I couldn't believe what I was hearing, I had gone to theatre expecting to be home a couple of hours later, and now I no longer had a womb and, from now on, would have to go to the toilet through a bag attached to my stomach. Despite being fuggy from the operation, the impact of the news was overwhelming and I instantly broke down in tears. I was angry, frightened, ashamed, in pain and consumed with self-pity.

In actual fact, I was lucky to be alive.

The original procedure was an endometrial ablation, which involves putting a balloon into your womb and filling it with hot fluid to scald the lining and stop the bleeding, but for some reason my uterus had split down the back so I was haemorrhaging and they needed to do a hysterectomy to save me. At the same time the scalding hot balloon had fallen through onto my bowel, causing devastating damage to the tissue.

But I found out the details later. For now, this night, all I could do was close my eyes and cry myself to sleep.

The following few days passed in a blur. I was usually such a strong independent woman and now I had to rely on either a nurse or Gina to wash me and wait for dressings or my colostomy bag to be changed. Eventually they were able to reduce the drugs and I could get out of bed with help, and the catheter and drips were taken away but I found it so hard to accept the colostomy bag. I wouldn't look at it for days. Through patient coaxing, my specialist stoma nurse, Stella, eventually persuaded me not only to look at the colostomy, but to care for it and change the bags myself.

Gina came to see me every day and on one occasion I complained that I couldn't wait to wash my hair. I have naturally curly hair that I straighten daily, otherwise it is just a frizz ball, so after about a week of lying in bed and not washing it, it was in a terrible state.

'Wash it then,' she said.

'I can't,' I replied, with tears in my eyes.

'Yes you can, we will do it together,' she smiled.

That's just what we did, or rather Gina did. She washed my hair, as I sat on a chair in front of the sink in the bathroom. I was still in so much pain that I could hardly lean forward, but Gina didn't mind, she gently emptied small cups of water over my head to wet my hair and rinse out the shampoo; it didn't matter that I was getting soaked, I had clean dry clothes in my locker, but Gina was getting wetter than me. I was aware of how gentle she was being with me, as though I was so fragile I would break. With my hair now washed and clean she dried it for me and then straightened it. It must have taken two or three hours as she had to keep stopping to let me have a breather, but she didn't complain, not once. I felt so much better, but the tears came again.

'I just want to go home,' I sobbed.

'I know,' she soothed. 'You can soon.'

I was missing my children more than words could say. Anni-Mae was still only a baby and couldn't come in to see me, though Marco and Millie had been to visit. I tried so hard to put on a brave face for them, but they both knew me too well and could see straight through me. I wanted more than anything to pull them close and cuddle them, but I was in too much pain, which upset me even further.

On one of the visits, Marco asked why I couldn't just come home.

'I want to so much but I can't, not just yet, mate,' I tried to reassure him.

'But why not?' he insisted.

I knew they needed to know what had happened as the recovery was going to be slow so I tried to explain as simply as possible that I had had an operation that meant I couldn't have any more babies and that because I had been so poorly the rest of my tummy was poorly too. I tried to paste on a big smile for them so they wouldn't worry, but they were both too bright to be fooled.

At long last, I was told I could go home. I had been in hospital for nearly three weeks and I was ecstatic! But my difficulties weren't over yet. As it happened, Kev was due to start a new job on the Monday after I came out of hospital and for six weeks he would be away on a residential training course Mondays to Fridays. I would be left alone. My family, Kev's parents Ann and Stuart, and all my friends were amazing, so I had plenty of support – but it was still very hard. I couldn't drive, I couldn't do any housework and, worst of all, Anni-Mae was just 16 months old and I couldn't even lift her up. I couldn't put her in the bath, let alone bend over to wash her.

Although aged just twelve and ten themselves, Marco and Millie really came into their own, and stepped up to the mark as big brother and sister. They made me drinks whenever I wanted one – and sometimes when I didn't – nag at me about having something to eat and they played with Anni-Mae, cuddled her if she was crying and even changed dirty nappies. My brother Mick would come daily to take the older two to school and drop Anni-Mae at nursery for me, then collect them all and bring them home again in the afternoon. Everyone rallied round helping with cleaning, shopping, all the day-to-day things that needed to be done.

And as usual, Gina was amazing. She would come over most days after work, even though she had her own family and Ashton was only 20 months old. Sometimes it was a flying visit so that she could see for herself that I was okay, other times she would bring over a casserole for us all to have for dinner and she would bathe Anni-Mae, put her to bed and ensure Marco and Millie didn't want for a thing. I really don't know how I would have got through that time without Gina and my other special friends – Hayley, Julie, Moira and Emma – as well as my wonderful family.

After a few weeks, I started to recover and could

go back to looking after my family myself, and get back to work, so Gina and I slipped back into our normal routine of meeting occasionally for lunch and spending weekends together doing stuff with the kids, and often with Kev and Shaun too.

However, for various reasons my relationship with Kev was starting to show cracks. I confided in Gina about everything in my life and this was no exception. She was very supportive when I told her my worries and reassured me she would always be there for me, no matter what happened.

In July, it was decided that the surgeon would attempt to reverse my colostomy. I thought I would be hugely relieved but it was a really tough decision for me. Naturally, I desperately wanted to get rid of this horrible bag, which was constantly attached to my side, dictating what I could do and what I could eat but, as a result of the last operation, I was terrified of what would happen once they had put me to sleep. I tried to get them to do it with a local or epidural but it couldn't be done, so I decided I had to face the fear and go for it anyway.

On the day of the operation, Gina came over to our house at about 6.30 in the morning, and double-checked my bag for the hospital as well as the clothes I had packed for Marco and Millie who were staying with my friend Moira. Anni-Mae was going to stay with Kev's parents. As Gina fussed around me she was constantly reassuring me, 'It will be fine, you will have your life back,' but I couldn't hide my fear from her any more than I could hide it from myself.

At the hospital, Gina sat in my room with me as we waited for the doctors to come – a rare occasion when Gina seemed lost for words – but her being there meant everything to me. She held my hand and promised that she would be there when I woke up, and then walked down the corridor with me as they took me to theatre. Back on the ward I awoke to be told everything had gone perfectly. And sure enough there was Gina sat by my bed, with Kev. Again the tears flowed, but this time it was relief.

Later that year, Kev and I decided to go our separate ways. It was sad, but for the best and luckily it was amicable. I found a house to rent and Gina and Shaun spent all day helping me move.

'We will soon have it feeling like home,' she grinned, and she was right. Our lives continued as normal only now I was a single mum again – but I never felt alone. Gina made sure of that.

Shortly afterwards I found a house to buy. I was elated. I could make this house a lovely home for me and the kids for as long as I wanted. Again, Gina and Shaun helped me every step of the way. I even went back to view the house a couple of extra times before I finally bought it so that Gina could cast her eye over it. I wanted her approval and her help to get it the way I wanted it.

In April 2008, we moved in. It was perfect. Marco and Millie argued playfully about who was having which room but we all soon felt at home in the new house. Gina helped me choose colour schemes and accompanied me on the many shopping trips needed for the curtains, carpets and all the other essentials. Shaun would come round to do all the 'men's jobs', as he put it. He joked that there was a law against Gina and I being allowed to use power tools so he, along with my brothers, hung curtain rails and pictures, and put up shelves whenever I needed them to.

• • •

One day in December, as I looked forward to the first Christmas in our new home, I made plans to go Christmas shopping with my friend Kaz. I got up and dressed as usual but I felt quite ill, with an agonising headache. I managed to take the kids to school and Anni-Mae to nursery, but when I got back home I climbed into bed again.

My phone ringing brought me round. I hadn't even been aware that I had fallen asleep.

'Where are you, you're late,' came Kaz's voice.

I went to answer her but I could barely lift my head off the pillow and the light from my phone screen was agony. My voice sounded muffled as I tried to talk to her.

'Jane? Jane?' Kaz said, sounding alarmed. And then, 'I'm on my way.'

Sure enough, Kaz arrived five minutes later. She took one look at me and immediately rang for an ambulance, then called my brother Mick and Gina. By the time the paramedics had rushed me to the hospital, Gina was already there. I vaguely remember the doctors doing a CT scan and a lumber puncture, then I was wired up to monitors and drips and drifting in and out of consciousness. For five days I was pretty much unconscious and extremely ill as doctors treated me for viral meningitis.

I don't remember much from those few days. On one occasion all my veins had shut down and the doctors were struggling to insert some drips, but with no success. I can recall Mick getting upset and Gina stood by the bed crying, and I have a hazy memory of her saying, 'Just leave her alone now.

Leave her alone.' She must have thought they were hurting me.

The first real memory I have once I started to recover is Gina feeding me rice pudding. Even though I was on the mend I couldn't eat because I felt so ill. I hadn't eaten in over a week, but I had a craving for rice pudding. Gina ran to the shop, bought a tin of rice pudding, then took it to the hospital kitchen and got them to heat it up, and she spoon fed me.

During my stay in hospital my friends and family once more rallied round to help, picking up the kids from school, making sure they were looked after and providing a constant stream of visitors, when I was strong enough to see them. When I came home, Gina was there to look after me and Marco, and Millie mucked in to help.

My being ill was hard on everyone, but one good thing did come out of it. It made me realise once and for all that Gina was the best mate a girl could ask for. I have never been more grateful to her – nor more aware of just how lucky I was to call her my best friend.

CHAPTER 4

A LOVE RENEWED

As the New Year dawned, Gina and I put our best foot forward and determined to make this our best year yet, putting all the health troubles of the previous twelve months behind us. We grabbed family and girly time together whenever we could, which as we had five children between us wasn't as often as we'd like, but it didn't matter. Life was good and I was happy.

Life was never dull with our two families and the five children continued to be close. Lewis and Marco could spend hours talking about the latest Xbox games and then challenging each other to onscreen duels. Anni-Mae and Ashton would squabble as toddlers do, but then we would often catch them holding hands while watching a favourite show on TV. And the difference in gender didn't matter to them at all. Anni-Mae would happily play with cars and trucks, just as Ashton would happily play with dolls. He was and still is fascinated by her long hair and he would sit and brush it for ages while they watched a film. Millie always fitted in anywhere, with the boys on the Xbox or with the little ones playing their games, but she was happiest sat in the middle of Gina and me. She was always grown up for her age and liked being one of the girls.

I missed Marco, Millie and Anni-Mae so much on the weekends they were with their dads, but spending time with Gina, Shaun and the two boys in their home filled the void a little. The constant hustle and bustle, the laughter and banter ringing through the house, warmed my heart. Lewis and Ashton treated me as one of the family and it was a pleasure chasing them through the house with their parents or playing games with them, hearing their little voices yelling out as we all had fun together.

Gina and I could spend all day in each other's pockets and then still spend hours on the phone in the evening. It had become a bit of a standing joke. We would time the phone call as it was free for an hour, so at 59 minutes we would end the call and then one of us would ring the other one back so it was free for a further hour.

We'd been known to sit on the phone to each other watching *EastEnders* and saying, 'I can't believe he's just done that!'

Shaun never got jealous of the relationship, although some men might have resented it. During the time they were separated, Gina and I had built up this huge friendship, and he always respected that. He worked all the hours God sent, including Friday and Saturday nights, and rugby took him out on Wednesday nights and Saturday afternoons, so I think, in fact, he appreciated that I was company for Gina.

As we were never off the phone, I wasn't surprised on a Wednesday night in 2009 when my phone rang and the caller display told me that it was Gina.

'Shaun's not well,' she said, then went on to explain that he had been to rugby training that night, just like every Wednesday, but he hadn't even managed to complete the warm up properly because he had been so out of breath. Shaun was such a fit and healthy man! He played sport regularly, didn't smoke and frequently went running so this was out of character for him.

'Maybe he has man flu?' I laughed. Gina giggled too.

'He's going to go to the doctor's tomorrow anyway,' she replied. 'He's probably brewing a chest infection or something.'

'Better to be safe than sorry,' I said, and we continued our conversation about this and that. No topic was too small for me and Gina to chat about. We chatted about everything, from whether we had got the sausages out of the freezer for tea, to our dreams and aspirations for our children.

Shaun went to see the doctor the following day and, as we expected, was put on antibiotics for a chest infection. Although he felt a bit under the weather, he wasn't really poorly and, not being one to give in to a sniffle, still went to work and carried on as normal. But at the weekend he still wasn't feeling any better so, as we sat round the table having lunch together, Gina and I suggested that he needed to go back to the doctor.

'Trust you,' Gina teased, light-heartedly. 'Anyone else would be happy with one lot of antibiotics but, noooo, you want to have an extra lot. You're just greedy.'

Shaun laughed and said that he would see how he felt over the next couple of days.

A few days later he did see the doctor again and the doctor was concerned enough to send him for a chest X-ray. 'Just routine,' she had explained. They felt that Shaun may have a touch of pneumonia, so they gave him some more antibiotics and sent him on his way, saying they would be in touch if anything untoward showed on the X-ray.

Shaun was sent to Glenfield Hospital in Leicester, and he hadn't even got out of the hospital car park on his way home when his GP rang and said, 'We need to see you immediately.' The X-ray had shown some fluid on his lungs, so they thought he had pneumonia and they wanted to do a chest drain to take the fluid off. His left lung capacity was down to the size of a closed fist, which was why he was so breathless. We were all concerned, but not overly so, as pneumonia in a young fit man is usually easily dealt with and they'd already been through it once with little Lewis so we thought we knew what to expect.

He was admitted immediately and had a chest drain inserted to get rid of the fluid and allow his lung to expand again. Although it's not a nice procedure Shaun felt the benefit of it immediately. The doctor also took some samples of the fluid and sent them to the lab, explaining that they wanted to test it for signs of cancer.

That thought hadn't occurred to Gina and it immediately set alarm bells ringing. She phoned me as soon as she could and explained what had happened. She sobbed down the phone to me, 'What if it's cancer?'

I tried to remain calm and reassure her that hopefully it was just the infection, but deep down I was terrified too.

Within a couple of days, they got the news of the results. That afternoon, I was pottering about in the kitchen having just got home from work when Gina called me at home, almost hysterical.

She sobbed down the line as she confirmed our fears. 'It's cancer.' But there was worse to come. She continued through her tears: 'It's terminal.'

Even though I had been worried, I still couldn't believe what I was hearing. Shaun? It couldn't be true, there must be a mistake! I couldn't find any words to comfort my best friend when it was obvious that her heart was breaking. I could see Marco and Millie playing out in the garden and, as Gina was speaking, I thought, 'How am I going to tell them Uncle Shaun is so poorly? More to the point, what about Lewis and Ashton? How will they take it? What will Gina and Shaun tell them?' So many questions were racing through my head but at that moment, the one thing I needed to do was get to my friend and be there for her. 'I'm on my way,' I managed to say.

I got in my car and drove straight to Gina and Shaun's home. Gina was there with her mum and dad as Shaun was still in the hospital. Gina sat on the sofa and I remember thinking that *she* looked like the one who was ill. She was deathly white, her eyes were swollen from crying and she was shaking from head to toe. I sat down next to her and she crumpled into my arms, sobs racking her body again. We sat there for quite some time. 'This isn't fair,' she kept saying. 'Why us?'

I didn't have an answer for her.

'This isn't what's supposed to happen,' she sobbed. 'We should grow old together, that's the normal thing to do. How can I tell Lewis and Ashton that their dad is dying? I can't lose him, Jane, I just can't!'

I felt awful because there was nothing I could say to make her feel better. All I could do was promise her that I would be there for her, for Shaun, and for Lewis and Ashton. I would help in any way that I could.

Eventually, I asked Gina how Shaun had taken the news.

She shrugged her shoulders. 'You know Shaun,' she said. 'He doesn't really say a lot.'

That was true. Shaun was a very private man.

Gina was trying to pluck up the courage to call Rich, who had been Shaun's best friend since they were toddlers and now lived in Holland. She wanted him to be one of the first people to know and had tried to call him but couldn't go through with it. 'If I tell Rich, it really is real,' she cried. I offered to make the phone call for her and, after speaking to Rich, I knew just what she meant. He was devastated and promised he would be over on the next available flight.

After some time sitting in her house, Gina handed me the leaflets that the hospital had given to her. Shaun had a type of lung cancer called adenocarcinoma, where the tumours are so small they are often described as 'ground glass', and they had been told that this type of cancer couldn't be cured.

The specialist said they would give Shaun chemotherapy to help prevent the cancer from growing or spreading. But even with chemotherapy, Shaun was looking at a grim prognosis. If he had the treatment, he might have six to nine months left. But the cancer would never be cured, even if the chemo gave him a little bit more precious time.

The treatment started immediately. He had CT scans so they could see the tumours, which don't show up on X-rays, then they had to drain the fluid out before they could start the chemotherapy due to the risk of infection. He needed to be as well as possible to withstand the treatment.

The next few days and weeks passed in a blur. I had promised Gina I would be there for her and her family and I was determined to make sure that I was. Sometimes I would accompany Gina to visit Shaun, other times I would have the boys while she went on her own. I would often drop her off at the hospital and then pick her up later to save on parking costs as I only lived a couple of miles away, whereas for Gina it was about an hour's round trip.

Shaun and Gina were allocated a nurse specialist named Angela, and what a very special lady she was! They introduced me to her and Gina would often ask me to accompany her to her updates with Angela as she was worried she would forget something that was said. Angela explained everything that Shaun would go though during his treatment and was always sympathetic and supportive, but it was often traumatic for Gina to hear what she had to say, no matter how diplomatically she put it.

Shaun took the diagnosis bravely but he could be stubborn and bloody-minded at times, and he really didn't want to accept how ill he was. He was still playing rugby, against doctor's orders, but his attitude was, 'If I'm dying, I want to do what I want to do while I still can.' Sometimes Gina would get exasperated with him and tell me, 'You go in and see him, he won't listen to me. You can get through to him!'

In the years since, a number of people have said to me that Gina would often say, 'I'm sending Jane in to him today, he will listen to her!' Or she'd tell them that she just needed a break and I was going in her place. It comforts me to know that she felt she could do that and I hope that in some way she found it a help.

One of these times was just before they took Shaun's chest drain out. The volume of fluid had been so great that it had split the outer membrane of Shaun's lung apart. Before removing the chest drain, the doctors had to inject a substance that would stick the lung back together and they explained that, while necessary, the procedure would be extremely painful. Gina couldn't face seeing Shaun in that much agony but couldn't leave him to face it alone so she asked me if I would go. I sat and held his hand throughout the whole procedure, as Shaun winced with pain. It felt like hours to me, so I can't imagine what it was like for Shaun. Eventually, it was over and after an X-ray they confirmed that it had been successful, and the chest drain could be removed, which would allow for the chemotherapy to begin.

As I was leaving the hospital that day, Shaun's brother David and his partner Lisa were just arriving. I remember us all having a cry in the corridor together but I honestly don't know who my tears were for – Shaun, Gina, myself, the family? I guess there were tears for everyone.

Gina and Shaun told different people as and when they were ready, and they had decided that they would be as honest with Lewis and Ashton as they could. Ashton was only four so he understood very little, he just knew Daddy wasn't feeling well. Lewis was ten so they used the word 'cancer' when they told him that Daddy was ill, but they only gave him the information that he asked for.

He never asked the question, 'Will you die?'

By a cruel twist of fate, Shaun's dad had also had lung cancer, and had had part of his lung removed, but it was a different type and he didn't need any chemotherapy. Lewis knew that granddad had had lung cancer and was now fine, so in his mind I suspect he may have been thinking, 'Daddy's going to be okay.' Sometimes, when Shaun was in hospital and Lewis was with me, he would ask, 'When will Daddy be better so that he can come home?' I didn't want to lie to him so I would say, 'Daddy's too poorly to come home yet but hopefully the doctors can make him feel better soon.' I was always careful to say make him *feel* better. We already knew that this was something that Shaun was never going to get better from.

• • •

I had to break the news to Marco, Millie and Anni-Mae, to whom Shaun was like a dad. Anni-Mae, like Ashton, didn't really understand, whereas Marco and Millie, at 15 and 13, knew exactly what it meant from seeing TV programmes and having lessons at school. They were devastated. It moved me so deeply that Marco cried, something that now he was in his teens he didn't do, at least not in front of me. I had expected tears from Millie but not from Marco. They both appeared quite angry, 'Why Shaun?' asked Marco. 'He doesn't smoke.'

I was so touched when they said, 'What about Lewis and Ashton, do they know? Is Auntie Gina okay? When can we see them?' They had so many questions, most of which none of us could answer.

I felt just as I had with Gina – helpless. It was horrible not being able to make it all better. I lost count of the number of times I wished that I had a magic wand.

After the initial shock Gina became very brave, at least for the most part, and especially in front of Shaun. I will always admire her for that. But there were times when we were alone that she would crumble. She felt cheated; it was all wrong, they were supposed to grow old together, supposed to see their boys grow up, marry, have children. They should have had their whole lives together and now that future had been snatched away. What could I say or do to make it any easier? Nothing! All I could do was be there for my friend and her family. Night after night, I wiped away Gina's tears and held her as she sobbed into my shoulder.

Shaun seemed to handle the news remarkably well – but how much of it was a front, I guess we will never know. One day, I was at their house when friends came to visit and a comment was made about how pale Shaun looked. Deadpan, Shaun simply replied, 'I am dying, you know.' They looked horrified, then Shaun burst out laughing. That was so typical of him, always the joker. Gina told him off and his friend gave him a playful smack and the visit continued with no feelings of awkwardness.

The chemotherapy regime was sorted out and commenced quickly. Shaun was to have chemotherapy every three weeks and there would be six treatments in total. Gina and Shaun always went out for a 'pre-chemo meal' on the Monday night before his treatment so they could spend some quality time together.

Shaun handled the chemotherapy brilliantly. On the day of chemo he would have to spend the whole day at the hospital as toxic drugs were pumped into him. Many people are sick and unable to get out of bed for days after the treatment, but he didn't let it hold him back. He was still going to work and he'd only have one day off after each dose, then he carried on life as normally as possible.

Gina and Shaun often popped into my house on the way home from the hospital as the route to hospital took them past my front door. On most treatment days, Shaun would walk in with a cheery, 'Get the kettle on then!'

'How ya doing?' I would ask, as casually as possible.

'You know me, strong as a bull,' he would laugh.

Occasionally, though, he would look drained and his normal sense of humour would be absent. Even for Shaun, there must have been times when it was too much for him to hide how he was truly feeling.

Although the chemo was a horrible thing to go through, Shaun made remarkable progress. The cancer was stable and he felt well in himself and he was put on Tarceva – the trademark name of erlotinib – an inhibitor drug that would hopefully continue to do what the chemotherapy had started by preventing the cancer cells from multiplying, keeping the cancer at bay. They caused a bright red skin rash that Shaun was very self-conscious about but they seemed to do the trick, so he wasn't about to let that bother him. Gina continued to be his rock, by his side at every appointment and constantly nagging him about taking his medication and looking after himself.

• • •

During this difficult time, life continued and we tried to snatch some fun and laughter wherever we could. My nephews were still racing sidecars and we would all go along to watch the meeting together. I had grown to love the sport too, so much so, in fact, I got my licence to be a passenger, which is not as passive a role as it sounds. Our job is not to sit demurely in a sidecar while the rider on the bike does all the work – it's much more dangerous than that. We are dressed in leathers and hanging off the sidecar to give the vehicle momentum when going round corners and negotiating tight bends. It can be pretty hairy at times, with bikes and sidecars flipping over if not handled properly.

One Wednesday when I was out for a day of practice at Mallory Park, a track that we were lucky enough to have just a few miles from our home, Gina came along to watch with Lewis and Ashton. I raced around, hanging out the side of the sidecar, the wind rushing past my helmet, and I could see Gina and the boys waving their arms madly at the side of the track cheering me on.

Towards the end of the session, as we came around one of the last corners travelling at 65 mph, I was feeling the strain of this exhausting physical sport. I shifted my hand across to get a better hold for the corner – and somehow managed to miss the hold.

A feeling of horror swept over me as I was thrown loose from the sidecar. The next thing I knew I was rolling over and over on the tarmac. I remember cursing as I was wearing my new helmet, and there was going to be no way it would get through this unscathed. I came to a stop, got my bearings and stood up.

My nephew had pulled the sidecar up some feet away down the track and I raised my hand to let him know I was all right, just as a marshal came running to my aid.

'Are you okay?' he shouted to me.

'I'm fine,' I answered. My arm and hand were hurting but not enough for anything to be broken and my backside was throbbing. The biggest injury was to my pride. I was so annoyed with myself.

My brother Mick and nephew came running down from the paddock as I walked across the track and once they had made sure I was all right, they had a bit of a laugh at my expense. I didn't mind, I was just miffed that I couldn't get straight back on.

As I got back to the racing van I could hear my mobile telephone ringing inside, I grabbed it and saw 'Gina' flashing on the screen. I answered it but before I could speak I could hear Gina crying. 'Is she okay? Is she hurt?' She was speaking so fast her words were falling over each other.

'Gina, it's me,' I said. 'I'm fine, calm down. I'm a bit bruised but nothing a hot bath won't solve.'

She switched from panic to telling me off. 'Don't ever do that to me again!' she shouted.

'Believe me, I never meant to,' I laughed.

'It's not funny,' she chastised, but I could hear the

relief in her voice and within a few seconds she was taking the mickey, along with my family.

'You're meant to hold on,' she laughed. 'That's the whole point of being a passenger!'

When I spoke to her later that evening on the telephone she said that it had looked very dramatic when I fell off. Apparently Ashton had turned round and very casually said, 'Well, I think Auntie Jane is dead.' Out of the mouths of babes, eh?

One weekend soon after, my nephews were competing at a British Superbikes meeting at Mallory Park and, unbeknown to Shaun, I'd made some phone calls and arranged for him to go and meet one of the big teams and get some signed memorabilia. We invited them to the race meeting to watch Stephen and Paul, which they gratefully accepted, especially as Shaun would get to see some of his idols race. When they arrived, we took them off to one of the top team's race lorries where they got to look at the bikes close up and meet the riders, one of whom, Richard Cooper, spent a lot of time talking to Shaun. He was given a team jacket, which the riders all signed, and he was really chuffed and very surprised. Everyone was very friendly and Gina and Shaun appeared to be having a ball.

It was quite a hot day and we were having a brilliant time but, as we walked down to the track to see my nephews' race, Shaun took his cap off to wipe the sweat from his forehead then looked down at his hand. It was covered in hair. He had been warned the chemotherapy would make his hair fall out so it had only been a matter of time but Gina and I just looked at each other, wondering what to say. It was a really awkward moment but Shaun took it all in his stride.

'Oh well,' he said with a smile on his face. 'It will make it easier not to shave.'

Once again, I marvelled at his bravery. I know full well if it had been me I would have been in bits, but that was Shaun all over. He just got on with it.

Both Gina and Shaun decided that they wanted to try and make a positive out of the situation and that they would throw themselves into fundraising. Naturally, I wanted to help in any way I could and so did everyone who knew them. Our friends Emma and Sharon held a cake stall for the Roy Castle Lung Cancer Foundation. Shaun's rugby team organised a car wash, T-shirts were made with the slogan 'support your local hooker' – the position that Shaun played – and we sold Livestrong wristbands. Shaun and his rugby friends even did a naked photo shoot for a team calendar – I still have one hanging proudly on my bedroom wall!

One of the biggest events was the coast-to-coast cycle ride that we organised in aid of the Roy Castle Foundation. And, boy, did it take some organising! We planned it for 27 July, Ashton's fourth birthday, and the team would cycle from Whitehaven to Sunderland, 135 miles in total, in twenty-four hours. We had to arrange transport to get the bikes to the starting point and to carry spare wheels and other kit, sort out accommodation for the night before and somewhere for us to stop for lunch so the lads could have a breather. David and Sally, some mutual friends, had family that lived in Consett, which was approximately halfway and they organised a local pub to provide refreshments for us when we arrived. The charity provided T-shirts and the people taking part trained for weeks before the event.

At last the day arrived. The lads hoping to complete the bike ride were Shaun's brothers, David and Andy, my nephew Stephen and Shaun's rugby teammates. Shaun himself was planning to complete part of the ride. Then we had a support crew made up of Shaun's dad, Mick, and Mel, the partner of one of the rugby lads, and me. John (or Oddjob, as he was more commonly known) would drive the van carrying spare wheels and other essentials, and we all had fluids, first aid kits and other gear in our cars.

We had an early start, up at 4.30 a.m. Gina would follow later with the kids once Ashton had opened his birthday presents, as would Lisa and Jenny, David and Andy's wives.

We got to the official starting point and everyone stood in a line on the beach, with the back wheels of their bikes in the water's edge. Then they were off! I cannot put into words the strength, pain and commitment of the riders on that day. Whenever people were struggling, they would offer words of encouragement to each other, shouting, 'Come on, this is for Buster,' which had been Shaun's nickname for many years. The bike ride was less than a week away from Shaun's last dose of chemotherapy and he had to be closely monitored due to the risk of infection, so I flagged him over every hour to take his temperature. Even so, he managed to complete around 85 miles of the ride himself, which showed an incredible amount of courage and determination.

At last we arrived at Consett for the much-needed pit stop. Gina had brought Ashton a cake and we all sang happy birthday as he blew out his candles. Then we were off again. All the riders were exhausted but no one was going to give up! When we got around ten miles from the end we agreed that the support team would go and wait for them at the finish line, where they would dip their front wheels into the water's edge to signify that they really had ridden from coast to coast. As we stood patiently waiting we saw the riding helmets just coming into view, then they all stopped.

'What on earth are they playing at?' Gina and I said to each other, but moments later they were on the move again. They had stopped to allow Shaun to get to the front of the pack and to make sure no one was left behind. As they rode down the promenade they were all together, with Shaun proudly leading them. Gina and the kids were punching the air, cheering loudly and clapping their hands, as were the whole crowd of friends and family. We were all so proud to be sharing that moment. Gina ran the last few feet to meet Shaun, then threw her arms around his neck, smothering him in kisses. It's fair to say that it was very emotional and I have never seen so many men shed tears. They had achieved what they had set out to do and had done it in a remarkable fifteeen hours!

I was and still am so proud to have been just a small part of that day.

• • •

A few days after the coast-to-coast cycle ride I was at Gina and Shaun's when Gina ushered me into the kitchen.

'I want us to renew our wedding vows' she whispered.

'Brilliant!' I said. 'What does Shaun think?'

'Well, I've briefly mentioned it in passing but I'm not sure whether he took me seriously. I thought you could ask him for me,' she giggled. 'I'm going shopping so do it now, while I'm out.'

As she spoke, she was gently pushing me into the lounge where Shaun sat and then I heard the front door shut. She really had gone to the shops and left me to it! I couldn't be annoyed because I knew how much this meant to Gina. In her eyes, their vows had been broken when they had separated for a short while, and now with Shaun being so ill and his life being limited renewing their vows meant everything to her.

At first, I sat down and had a bit of a chat with Shaun about nothing in particular. 'How the hell am I supposed to approach this one?' I thought to myself. Then I took a deep breath and said, 'You know Gina wants to renew her wedding vows?'

Shaun peered over his mug of tea at me.

'She has mentioned it,' he said calmly.

'Well, what do you think?' I asked, with my fingers crossed in my lap.

'Is it really that important to her?' he replied.

I nodded and smiled saying, 'You know it is.'

'Fine,' he said, happily. 'If that's what she wants, let's do it. But you two can sort it out. Just tell me where to be and what time.'

I was thrilled. And just a short time later, I heard Gina come back. She tentatively put her head around the lounge door, out of sight of Shaun. I put my two thumbs up and she shrieked, then she went over to Shaun and gave him the biggest hug. 'Thank you, babe, it means so much to me.'

He hugged her back and repeated, mischievously, 'Just sort it out and tell me where I have to be and when.'

Not a problem for Gina – she couldn't wait to get started on the arrangements.

From then on it was all go. She chose the date of 30 August 2009, just a few weeks away. Gina and Shaun agreed that, as well as a celebration of their love, it also would be a fundraising event so it was decided that rather than the traditional reception they would have a fun day. There was so much to do and to arrange but the excitement of it all just carried us along.

Gina had never really had a proper hen night when she and Shaun had originally got married, so Emma and I decided to make up for it this time round – and then some! We told Gina we were just arranging a quiet meal in a local restaurant and asked who she would want to be there, then we started planning, all without Gina having a clue. To this day, I have no idea how we managed it because she was so nosey.

The night arrived, we had decorated the restaurant and the table, and my niece had made fortune cookies with a pretty little tag saying 'Gina's night' attached to them. We brought an array of the usual hen night stuff – pink fluffy L-plates, shot glasses on a necklace, that sort of thing. We had dreamed up a forfeit for every guest, which they could present to Gina throughout the night. When Gina arrived she burst into tears. She really had no idea, but at least this time they were tears of happiness.

We had a great time in the restaurant but soon it was time to leave for the other pubs in town. Gina got presented with one of her forfeits, which was to 'travel in style'. No, we hadn't booked a limo, it was a spacehopper – the big orange ball with a face on it, which you sat on to bounce along. Tonight that was Gina's mode of transport. She took it all in her stride and bounced all the way through Loughborough town centre to the shouts of onlookers and car horns being beeped at her, but she really didn't care! There were lots of other forfeits including wearing a pair of 'granny' shoes that Emma had found in a charity shop – Gina loved that one because her feet were hurting in her high heels – plus she had to wear the biggest pair of pants we could find on the market, a pair of beige Y-fronts. Gina duly pulled them on over her posh outfit and took many more forfeits with a giggle. That was Gina all over. She was out to enjoy life and never gave a hoot what anyone thought of her.

After a few drinks in the pub, we were going to go on to a club. Gina stood in the pub, chatting away with a drink in her hand and she was having a great evening. Last orders were called and then the bouncers moved in to say, 'Drink up, ladies. Time to go.' Suddenly, I saw Gina freeze and the glass just slipped out of her hand. I knew exactly what she was thinking. We had been in so many pubs where it would be Shaun on the door, saying, 'Come on, you two. Drink up. It's kicking out time.' As the glass hit the floor, she just turned and ran, so I tapped Emma on the shoulder and we ran after her. I caught up with her outside and she was sobbing. I put my arms around her just as her legs went out from under her. Emma and I both held her. Her heart was breaking in front of me. It was devastating to see her like that.

• • •

Finding the perfect outfit for the day was never going to be easy as Gina's self-critical streak always emerged when she was trying clothes on. Emma and I decided that when we took Gina shopping for her vows renewal dress we would make it a day to remember, and it definitely was. Gina wasn't even sure what colour she wanted to wear, let alone what style, so we went in countless shops and she tried on numerous dresses, but she was never one hundred per cent happy with any of them. The assembly of the whole outfit was getting a bit back to front. She bought shoes, a necklace, even a dainty band for her hair. She also wanted some Bridget Jones style 'hold-me-in pants' so Emma and I found the most garish ones in the shop and then had to go into Gina's changing room and try to pull them up for her, which none of us could do for laughing so much! At one point, Gina fell over onto her bum as she tried to get herself into them and she grabbed the changing room curtain as she went down, yanking it open for all to see. We laughed hysterically and I caught the whole thing on camera.

We had a ball of a day but as time was getting on Gina looked sad.

'I'm never going to find anything to wear,' she said wearily.

'Yes, you will,' Emma and I chorused.

'We can go to Nottingham at the weekend if we have to, and we will find you the dream dress,' I added.

As we were walking back to the car, I noticed a dress in the window of the Laura Ashley shop. We hadn't been in there as it wasn't a shop that any of us would normally enter, but the colour had caught my eye – such a deep, rich pink. It was made from a material that flowed so beautifully, it really did look like liquid. It was floor length, with a band around the middle, and above that it flowed up over the shoulders, giving the bodice a dramatic V neckline. I pointed out the dress to Gina and we marched straight in.

The sales assistant explained that it was the last dress and it was a size 10. Gina's face crumpled; she was a size 12.

'Try it on anyway,' Emma and I coaxed. Gina reluctantly disappeared into the changing room and re-emerged from it a minute later looking absolutely beautiful. The dress fitted perfectly and the colour looked gorgeous on her. Emma and I both had tears running down our cheeks. There is only one word to describe how Gina looked: stunning.

'Do you think Shaun will like it?' she asked, suddenly unsure.

'He'll love it,' I replied 'But then again, Shaun would love you in a bin bag.'

It was the perfect end to a perfect day. My best friend was happy and that's all I could ask for.

A few days later, over a cup of tea and a table full of plans for the big day, Gina said, 'Remember you said you would do anything for us?'

'Of course,' I said, a little warily. What could she have in mind?

'Well, there is one thing,' she said, with a playful smile. When she told me her plan I laughed.

'Of course. I would love to help!'

It was going to take some organising but if that was what my best friend wanted then that was what she was going to get!

• • •

At last the big day arrived. A friend had borrowed an old Jaguar car and I had had ribbons and bows made for it. Shaun knew about the car, but Gina didn't have a clue and apparently her face was a picture when he turned up to collect her. My nephew Paul was a photographer and had agreed to take pictures for them. Lewis and Ashton looked the part in their black trousers and waistcoats, with silver ties that matched their dad's. The guests filed in to the church and took their seats, with some standing because the church was full to bursting.

As Gina arrived, sixteen of us stood up and walked to the back of the church. The gathered guests, including Shaun, turned round in confusion. Then the music started to play – The Whispers' disco classic 'It's a Love Thing' – and we all put huge sunglasses on our heads and started dancing down the aisle towards a bewildered Shaun. We had practised the dance time and time again, wanting to make sure it was right for their big day. We kept the moves simple and we all stayed perfectly in time with each other, including Gina. I don't know how she managed it. I would have been too nervous to remember what I was supposed to be doing. After a few bars, even the vicar was bobbing along! The dance ended with Gina walking down the middle of us with a huge grin on her face. Everyone was laughing, singing and clapping along and I squeezed her hand as she got to Shaun, who was beaming with pride.

The ceremony went perfectly, although it was very emotional. Gina and Shaun didn't take their eyes off each other throughout the service, nor did they let go of each other's hands, their fingers entwined throughout. They obviously gave each other a huge amount of strength as not once did they falter or their voices crack. I, on the other hand, cried copious tears, and as I looked around at the other guests in that church, I knew that I was not the only one.

As the service neared its end, Gina had her own surprise in store for me. She turned and beckoned me with her finger.

'Do you want Paul to take some more photographs?' I asked. She shook her head and beckoned to me again. As I stood the vicar said that he now wished for Gina and Shaun's witnesses to come forward. Now I knew what she wanted. She hadn't mentioned it but Gina had chosen me to be one of the witnesses while Shaun had chosen his long-term friend, Rich. I was truly, truly honoured!

After the ceremony had finished and hundreds of photographs had been taken, we headed back to the local pub for the reception and fun day. A lot had been arranged, from tombola stalls to raffles, a bucking bronco and a huge auction for which we had managed to get, among numerous other items, signed memorabilia from the Leicester Tigers rugby club, signed photographs of Italian motorcycle champ Valentino Rossi, as well as a studio day, where someone could be a presenter at Oak FM, our local radio, with all the proceeds going to charity. We raised over £12,000 on the day.

Gina made a speech and thanked everyone for being there, not just for that day but supporting them both since the devastating news about Shaun's illness. Gina had sent a text around to friends and family a few days beforehand asking people to sum up Shaun in one word and she read some of these out. The same words came up time and time again: inspirational, strong, brave, a legend. Gina was obviously very emotional and I was so proud as I stood and listened to her words.

Next Shaun spoke, again thanking everyone for their support, thanking Gina for being his rock, and then, having had rather a lot to drink, he led the rugby lads into a rousing chorus of 'Swing Low, Sweet Chariot'. That was too much for me and Emma and we burst into tears. Gina came to join us and we stood huddled together as the rugby lads got louder and louder then, suddenly, Shaun stripped down to his boxer shorts for his turn on the bucking bronco, saying that his trousers were too slippy. Gina couldn't stop giggling at his comical attempts to keep his balance and cling on for dear life.

Despite what Gina and Shaun were going through they spent the whole day joking and laughing. I really was in awe of their courage. They spent most of the afternoon and evening together, but whenever they got separated as they were circulating, you could see them looking around for one another. Ashton and Lewis remained glued to their mum and dad throughout – in fact, the only time that Gina intentionally let go of Shaun's hand was to hug her boys.

As I watched them together, united as an invincible duo, I reflected that they didn't need to renew their vows to show how much love they had for each other. That was obvious for all to see.

CHAPTER 5

BROKEN HEARTS

After that special day, Shaun's treatment continued. Gina would always attend hospital appointments with him, and would sit with him as the chemotherapy was given through a drip in his hand. She spent hours online researching anything that might make Shaun feel better and was constantly making disgusting smoothies with things like broccoli and beetroot that she had read would be good for him. The smell alone turned my stomach, so goodness knows how they made Shaun feel when he was already nauseous as a side effect of the chemotherapy! But he always laughed about it and tried them, to make Gina happy, then tipped them down the sink as soon as she wasn't looking!

Shaun had to stay in hospital a couple of times due to minor infections, but on the whole he was doing extremely well.

As Shaun's chemotherapy sessions were drawing to an end, he was looking well. The evening before he was due to attend hospital for his last dose, Gina arranged for all their family and friends to be waiting at the pub for their customary 'pre-chemo meal'. As they walked in a huge cheer went up from all of us and Shaun was visibly surprised but absolutely delighted. During the course of the evening Gina and Shaun again thanked everyone for their help and support. At one point I was wondering how they coped so well, then I smiled to myself as I realised the answer was obvious. They had each other!

The scan at the end of the treatment confirmed that the chemotherapy had stopped the cancer growing – for now. Both Shaun and Gina knew that there wasn't a cure but in relative terms, this was the best news they could have hoped for. Gina phoned me as soon as they arrived home from the hospital to tell me the news. She was elated and I was so pleased for them both, yet there was a tinge of apprehension. How long would this good news last?

114

Despite the relief in Gina's voice, I feared for my friend and her family, and just what the future would bring them.

• • •

Christmas 2009 came and went with the usual hustle and bustle – too much food and wine, and spending too much money. One thing that being around Gina and Shaun had taught me was that life is too short for stress and anxiety. It's best to cherish each moment and enjoy it to the full. That's just what Gina and Shaun did, even though there was a chance that he wouldn't be there for the following Christmas. They made the most of everything.

It was over the festive period that they decided they needed a truly memorable family holiday with Lewis and Ashton. They had already missed out on the Caribbean when Gina was pregnant with Ashton, so they wanted to splash out on another dream destination and this time they settled on Mexico. As usual, it became an all-consuming mission for Gina and she researched everything to make sure it was a holiday they would never forget.

And the vacation wasn't the only excitement. Shaun had decided it was time for a change of hobby. While he was managing to go to work each day, and at his hospital appointments they continued to be amazed at how well he was doing, he had come to the conclusion – with a little help from Gina – that he was getting too many knocks in rugby and he opted to hang up his boots. As a (much) younger man he had been into motocross – motor biking cross country – so naturally he went back to racing bikes. It was something he could share with his brother David, so every weekend they would pack up the van and off they would go for couple of days. Initially, Gina didn't really see how this dangerous sport was better than rugby, but if it was something that Shaun really wanted to do, she reasoned calmly, who was she to stand in his way? She gave him her full support and started going off to meetings with him.

Trust Gina and Shaun to turn it into a production, however. At the first proper meeting that Shaun entered, I phoned Gina every hour for an update. She made me laugh when she told me that for his first race he gave the bike too much throttle at the start gate – and promptly fell off the back onto his backside!

I tried to go along with them as often as I could, but my weekends were fairly full with dropping off and picking up my children at their dads', so I couldn't attend if the meetings were too far away.

If I wasn't with them, I looked forward to Sunday evenings when Gina would call me for a lowdown of what the weekend had entailed for them all. Even though I couldn't be there as often as I had liked, it was great to see Gina and Shaun sharing something that made them so happy. Even Lewis and Ashton got into it and Shaun brought them their own little bikes and kits so they could have a go.

As well as family events, Gina and I would still meet up regularly for our girly time – though not nearly as much as we would have liked. And circumstances were against us. In late 2009 Gina and I had been told that the Charnwood site of AstraZeneca would be closing and people would be made redundant. We were both gutted. My department was one of the first to go and, in November that year, I started a new job at a GP's surgery. I really enjoyed the job and my colleagues were friendly but I missed AstraZeneca and, more importantly, I missed my lunchtime rendezvous with Gina.

But for now Gina's job was safe – so she stayed on.

• • •

Before we knew it, it was time for Gina and Shaun to be away on their dream holiday. The day before she left she came to visit and, as I waved her off at the door, there was a hollow feeling in my chest. I was hurting for my friend and the uncertain future that lay ahead of her. The constant feeling that there was nothing I could do ate me up inside.

I couldn't wait for Gina and her family to be home; I missed all of them enormously. Two weeks felt like a lifetime. They arrived back full of life with glowing tans and bursting with stories. They really had had the time of their lives and I couldn't have been more pleased for them. I leafed through the hundreds of photographs Gina had taken over the fortnight. She had wanted to capture every moment. If you didn't know them you would never have guessed the tragedy behind their smiles.

But it seemed they weren't the only ones with trouble on their hands. Around this time, a close friend of mine was diagnosed with lymphoma, or blood cancer. When he was very ill there were times that I helped to nurse him. Gina was always there for him and me, even though she had so much at home to cope with. In time my friend made a complete recovery and I'm very pleased to say that he is still doing well to this day. I could tell that Gina and Shaun were genuinely pleased that he came through the cancer, in spite of Shaun's contrary prognosis. I'm not sure I could have been as selfless and generous about it as they were. I'd like to think I would be, but honestly, I suspect I would have been bitter at the unfairness and randomness of this terrible disease, which allows some people to get better while others never would.

Throughout Shaun's illness both Gina and Shaun were gracious, and always grateful for what they did have, never resentful of other people. Naturally, Gina had days when she would feel angry and upset and ask herself 'Why us?' – and she had every right to feel that way because all her future dreams had been shattered – but on the whole they made the most of everything while they still could.

With the dream holiday over Gina and Shaun continued as a normal family, going to work as usual, while Lewis and Ashton carried on at school. There was no outward sign of the tragedy that had struck the little family and the turmoil that their lives were in, or the big black cloud hanging over them that never dissolved between the hospital appointments. Although Shaun seemed healthy to all around him, the prognosis was never far from their thoughts and they knew they were living on borrowed time.

One night, when Shaun had gone out for a while with some friends, Gina and I were having a girly night in and chatting away as usual. The time seemed right to broach a question that I had been hesitant to ask, so I decided to just come out with it.

'Gina,' I said gently. 'How will you cope, babe, when the time comes?'

It probably wasn't the most tactful of questions but I genuinely feared for my friend. Gina and I always spoke openly and honestly about things, and I couldn't just tell her everything was going to be okay because we would both have known that I was lying. Besides, in her darker moments, I know she had thought about how she would cope without Shaun by her side, how she would have to carry on for the sake of the boys, and how she would have to be as strong as she could.

Her answer was short and simple.

'I will probably lock myself away in my bedroom with you for a few days,' she said. 'And then I will just get on with it, because you will make me. You won't let me slide into a black hole that I can't get out of. You will keep me going!'

She was right. I would be there for her and get her through it. The problem that was I really didn't know how I was going to do that. I would just have to figure that out when the time came. I knew I would do whatever was necessary.

• • •

As well as worrying about my best friend, I was also concerned about my sister Ann and her family. Ann's husband, my godfather Brian, was very ill with motor neurone disease and, as his condition worsened, Ann was getting increasingly run down with the strain of looking after him. I couldn't help thinking if this was how it was going to be for Gina in the future.

I did whatever I could to help Ann and Brian as well as being there for my niece Sam and my nephews Justin, Neil and Lee. They were all grown up but, like Lewis and Ashton, they were going to lose their dad some time soon. However old you are, it's a completely devastating loss.

Despite her own immense troubles, whenever I went round to their house, my sister never failed to ask after Gina and Shaun, and ask me to pass on her love. She was such an inspiration to me.

As the next phase of the AstraZeneca site closure was imminent, Gina started applying for jobs in the summer of 2010. I knew that she would have no difficulty finding a new position as she was so good at what she did and people thought highly of her. She could afford to be choosy about which job she decided to take and she was genuinely pleased when she was offered a job with a large company in Nottingham. The only thing she was worried about was the 25-mile round trip every day and, as I had done the same journey for six years in my previous job, she asked me how I found it. I explained it was a bit of a bind but you just got used to it. In hindsight, I wish I had said it was awful and not to take the job, that it was too far to travel. But after an emotional farewell to her friends and colleagues at AstraZeneca, she had a short break then started at her new job.

She called me on the Monday evening after her first day in her new role and she was really happy and chirpy. Everyone had been really nice and friendly, she told me, and the journey hadn't been as bad as she was expecting. Most importantly, she had had a long conversation with her new boss and she had explained in more detail about Shaun's condition and how her family life revolved around his cancer. He had been very understanding and compassionate, reassuring Gina that she could be there for her husband as much as she wanted to be, and could work from home whenever necessary. She was so relieved. Underscored by everything that had happened to her lately, Gina's philosophy was that you 'worked to live, not lived to work', so her boss's understanding was incredibly important to her.

I didn't get to see Gina for the rest of that week, due to her new job and my own shift-work. I had my usual nightly phone conversations with her, but that's just not the same as a face-to-face natter and a hug when you say goodbye. Nevertheless, I could tell she was enjoying the new job and it was lovely to hear her so happy after everything she'd been through. The following Monday, Gina rang after work again, to fill me in on their weekend of motocross. She chatted light-heartedly about how Shaun got on in his race and the fact that it had been so cold. I remember smiling to myself as I imagined Gina wrapped up in several layers of clothing, with a pom-pom hat on her head.

Our conversation veered to the following weekend and our Friday evening plans – wine, face masks, nail polish and great company. I couldn't wait! As we said our goodbyes, she said, 'I won't speak to you tomorrow as you're on the late shift, so we'll speak on Wednesday.'

'Sure will,' I replied.

'Love ya, babe,' she said.

'Love ya too' I replied, the usual way that our phone calls would end.

• • •

The next morning, Tuesday, I roused myself with a groan. Tuesdays had always been my least favourite day because of the late shift. But moaning about it wouldn't make it go any quicker. That day, 12 October 2010, I arrived at the clinic as usual and, to help put a smile on my face, made myself think of the girly night that Gina and I had planned that Friday.

Shortly after two, my mobile phone rang and the caller display told me that it was Gina's mum. My first thought was, 'Why on earth would Gina's mum be ringing me at work?'

I picked up the phone. 'Hello you,' I said, in a light-hearted, breezy voice.

Nothing could have prepared me for what I was about to hear.

It was instantly apparent that she was crying and my thoughts flew automatically to Lewis and Ashton.

'What's happened? Are the boys okay?' I asked frantically.

'It's not the boys,' she wept.

'Then what?' I asked. My heart was in my mouth and I felt physically sick.

'It's Gina,' she said.

Racked with sobs, she couldn't say any more. She passed the phone to Gina's dad.

'She has been killed in a car crash,' were the only words he could get out through his tears.

I couldn't speak. My phone crashed to floor as tears rolled down my face. I couldn't believe what I was hearing. My beautiful, loving, amazing friend was gone, wiped out in an instant.

My world shattered and I simply fell apart. My colleague came straight over to comfort me but I was lost for words. Stunned. She called my brother Mick, then put me in her car to get me home.

I vaguely remember my phone ringing again as I was on the way home. SHAUN flashed up on the screen. My stomach lurched. I felt like my heart had been shredded, so I couldn't even begin to imagine how Shaun was feeling, or the boys. I just kept saying to my colleague all the way home, 'The poor boys. What about the boys?'

As I sat staring at my telephone screen, with Shaun's name flashing on it, I couldn't find the strength to press the answer button. I was a coward, but I didn't know what to say to him. At this point I was still in my colleague's car and it was not a conversation I wanted with an audience so

I chickened out. I decided I would call him back once I was home and had checked on my own three children or, even better, I would get to him as quickly as possible as I felt actions would speak louder than words. I knew that there was nothing that I could think to say that would be of any comfort to him.

At home, I found Mick waiting. By this time Marco and Millie were home from school, and my brother had broken the terrible news to them. They were in pieces. Mick told me later that they had guessed something was wrong when they arrived home from school to find him there and, as he had also built up a good friendship with Gina and Shaun, they could see he was visibly shaken. They had panicked, assuming something had happened to me, so he had been forced to tell them. In truth, I was relieved that I didn't have to form the words myself. I'm not sure I could have got through the sentence.

'Are you sure it's Auntie Gina?' they both asked. They didn't want to believe it any more than I did. They loved her like a second mum.

Mick knew Gina's dad as they lived on houseboats that were moored close to each other, so I asked Mick to call him back. I'd been so upset that I had just dropped my phone on hearing the news without even saying goodbye. Mick spoke to him and passed on his condolences, then said I wanted to apologise for my reaction but Gina's dad said he completely understood.

'She wants to come over to be with Shaun and the boys,' said Mick.

'She doesn't need to ask,' he replied.

When I arrived at the house, Shaun was just letting a friend out of the door. As the friend walked away, I looked Shaun in the face and he looked like a lost little boy, so sad and helpless. It felt like I was moving in slow motion. I went straight over to Shaun and held him. 'I can't believe it. I was supposed to go first,' he kept saying, over and over.

As I walked through the door, the first thing that hit me was the sound... absolute silence. Nothing. It was so quiet. This house had always been full of laughter, chatting, even children being told off. Now there was nothing but the low whisper of the people that had gathered in the kitchen, all in a state of shock.

I asked after Lewis and Ashton, and went to the lounge where they both were. The television was on but both boys looked as though they were staring through the screen rather than watching the programme. Being just five years old, Ashton was totally confused by the house full of people, and being told his mum was gone. He chatted to me about nothing in particular then simply said, 'My mum has died.'

'I know, darling,' I comforted him as best I could. 'But she will now be an angel and live in the brightest star in the sky.'

Next, I went over to sit with Lewis and see how he was doing. He was 11, and bewildered by the day's events. He was trying to be brave but you could see in his eyes that his heart was breaking.

People were coming and going so I helped the boys get ready for bed, and made tea and coffee – all on autopilot. When people starting thinning out I asked Shaun if he wanted me to stay that evening to help with the boys. He said he did so I told him I would be back later and I went home briefly to spend some time with my own children so I could comfort and reassure them.

I had got just them all settled in bed when my phone rang. It was Shaun, asking me to bring my vacuum cleaner when I went back to his house. He had just snapped the belt on his own and he was devastated because he had promised Gina he would hoover that night when he got home from work, and he didn't want to let her down.

Shaun and I sat in silence that evening. I did manage to get him to eat a sandwich with a cup of tea, but we were both lost in our own thoughts and there wasn't really anything to say. Nothing could change the fact that our worlds had been shattered.

After Shaun had gone to bed, I lay on the sofa but there was no way I was going to get any sleep. Every time I closed my eyes I saw Gina's beautiful face and heard her infectious giggle. I couldn't believe that the only time I would see her now was when I remembered the many good times we had spent together over the years, but now no new memories could ever be made.

That was the longest night I have ever known.

• • •

The following morning a few family and friends were going to visit the site of the crash, but I didn't want to go. I didn't want to see the place my best friend had taken her last breath.

We slowly pieced together what had happened. Gina had been travelling along a steeply undulating road – known to locals as 'Roller-coaster Road' because of its peaks and troughs – when she collided with another car, driven by a young man coming in the opposite direction. There was nothing that she could have done to avoid the crash. She died at the scene, as did the other driver. I was told that her death would have been instantaneous, but even so I couldn't stop thinking that she had been alone and frightened, and I hadn't been there for her.

Shaun had to go back to the hospital to collect some paperwork and see Gina. I went with him, along with Gina's parents, Gina's sister Keri and her husband Mike, Shaun's brother David and his wife Lisa. We sat in a cold, stark little room while someone went through the formalities of the paperwork, then we were told we could see her. Shaun went in first on his own, the rest of us taking our turn after him.

My beautiful friend was lying in a hospital gown. This broke my heart as she had always hated them. Her hair had been washed and it had gone curly – another thing she hated – so I ran my fingers through it, trying to straighten it, and adjusted her fringe, which was out of place. All the time I was talking, telling her, 'This isn't funny, wake up, come back.'

'Life doesn't work without you in it,' I said, but obviously I got nothing back, I could barely breathe and the hurt was indescribable. I hugged her and held her hand – I have no idea how long for but when I moved away I saw that my tears had left a wet patch on her gown.

'Sorry,' I said. 'I've snotted on you now!'

She would have laughed at that if she could have heard me. But my beautiful, loving, amazing best friend had gone, and taken the laughter with her.

Eventually I had to leave, and my last words to her were, 'You're a beautiful angel now, babe. Spread your wings and fly...'

PART TWO

CHAPTER 6

FAREWELL, MY FRIEND

The days after the accident passed in a blur of activity. It was busy, because there was so much to do, but at the same time, everything seemed to move in slow motion. Shaun was lost. I tried to give him direction and support, as did Gina's parents, his own family and friends and his rugby teammates, but he was struggling with his overwhelming grief.

The toughest thing to tackle was the funeral arrangements. Shaun knew that he had to ring the funeral director's and he got as far as typing the number into his phone a couple of times, then went to put the phone to his ear and changed his mind. Eventually he held the phone out to me. He didn't need to put it into words, I knew what he was asking, so I simply nodded my head, took the phone and walked out into the garden. If I really had to make that call, I needed to be alone.

The funeral director Suzanne was a lovely lady and I explained to her that Shaun hated Gina being in the hospital. He felt she was alone and, at the very least, he wanted her back in the village. Suzanne promised me that she would get Gina home as soon as possible. I was really touched that She had referred to it as 'bringing her home'. It was only a small detail but it meant so much to hear. I arranged for Shaun to go and see her the following day so that he could talk through the arrangements, and he asked me if I would come along with him for moral support.

We all continued to rally round, thinking of the practical things that would need to be done. I knew Shaun would need a lot of help so I took some time off work. I wouldn't have been much use there anyway, consumed as I was with thoughts of Gina and her family. We made a list of telephone calls that would need to be made, made sure Shaun and the boys were eating, and made tea and coffee for the never-ending stream of visitors who dropped in to pay their respects. The amount of support was overwhelming and the sheer number of visits, calls, texts and sympathy cards was unbelievable. Shaun kept Gina's Facebook account active as the messages and tributes being written on her wall were all so affectionate and moving. A message was never posted informing friends of her tragic death, but word soon got round that this vibrant person, so loving and full of life, had been taken away from us. An actual tribute page was also created. To this day we don't know who did that. It is still an open page and people continue to write on both this page and Gina's Facebook wall.

The reason for this outpouring was easy to understand. Gina was an amazing, warm, loveable lady who was loved by so many people, and this love extended to the three people that mattered to her most: her husband Shaun and their two wonderful little boys.

The following day Emma took the boys out for a few hours while Shaun and I went to the funeral director's. As we sat discussing the plans, I felt oddly detached, as if I wasn't really in the room. I didn't want to believe it was really happening.

The design we chose for the order of service and the memorial cards showed footprints in the sand, and we gave Suzanne the words that we wanted to go into the newspaper. Shaun chose a white coffin with silver handles and plaque, and he was asked if there was anyone in particular that he would like to carry Gina into church. He looked over at me with a questioning face and I asked Suzanne if she could give us a minute alone.

'Of course,' she replied, gently placing a hand on Shaun's shoulder. 'I'll go and make us all a cup of tea, just take your time.'

I really didn't know how to approach what I was about to say to Shaun. Gina and I had had a number of conversations over the last year about what would happen when Shaun slipped away and she asked me to write down certain details that she wanted, and to keep the list somewhere safe so that when the time came, if she fell to bits, things would still be done the way she wanted them. One of these conversations had included the pallbearers, and she had chosen a few of his closest friends, who were her friends too.

Shaun sat still as I told him what we had talked about and, when it came to the pallbearers, I crouched down in front of him and took his hands, so I could look into his eyes. In response, he looked at me, sadly, and nodded.

'That's who I want to carry her then,' he said. 'She's chosen them for herself.'

Just then Suzanne returned with a tray of drinks and I passed the names on to her. Suzanne explained the other details that we would need to finalise and we said goodbye. As we left the funeral parlour, my whole body felt heavy with tiredness, I was emotionally drained. Shaun's own devastation must have felt even more overwhelming. I honestly don't know how he managed to put one foot in front of the other.

Despite his crushing grief, however, Shaun was bearing up admirably and he was doing an amazing job of looking after the two boys. Health-wise, he had been doing so well for so long on the inhibitor drug that people had seemed to have forgotten that he was ill. Despite his initial prognosis in the summer of 2009 that gave him only six to nine months to live, over a year later there were no signs of change in him. He'd completed the treatment, his hair had grown back and he was still working, so it was easy to forget he was poorly.

He was a brave, proud man but every now and again, usually when he was alone with me, or with me and Emma, his exterior would crack and the tears would flow. I couldn't find any words of comfort because there really weren't any, so we would just hold his hand, let him know that he wasn't alone and that we would always be there for him and the boys.

After our appointment with Suzanne, I went with Shaun to the supermarket to get some essentials. We pulled up on to his drive and as I was lifting some of the shopping bags out of the boot, I heard Shaun say my name. I peered around the car at him.

'What's up?' I said.

'Would you speak at Gina's funeral?' he asked me. I hadn't been expecting that.

'I... I... I'm not sure,' I stammered in reply.

'You don't have to,' he reassured me. 'But it would mean so much if you did. I can't think of anyone that Gina or I would rather have do it than you.'

I nodded my head slowly. 'I'm so honoured. I will try, but I can't promise,' I said, my voice breaking.

Shaun asked me and Emma to be there when the vicar came to talk to him about the funeral service and we reassured him that we would be at his side every step of the way. Chris, the vicar, was a lovely man, putting us all at ease as much as he could under the circumstances. After chatting about Gina, her work, the sort of mother and wife she was, and gathering a few stories from us, he asked the three of us to give him a couple of words or a phrase we felt best described her. Shaun simply said, 'She was my rock.' I said 'beautiful smile', and Emma said 'bubbly'. That made us all laugh because Gina hated being described as bubbly. She always thought it was a polite way of saying that someone on the large side was happy, as in 'big and bubbly', so Emma changed the word to 'vivacious'.

We chose the hymn together and Shaun said he wanted Gina to leave the church to 'their song', Starship's 'Nothing's Gonna Stop Us Now', which we all agreed was a fitting choice. Then Chris asked if there was any music that Shaun would like as Gina was brought into the church and, lost, he looked over towards me and Emma. As Gina loved Robbie Williams, I suggested 'Angels', and we all agreed, then Chris took the final details, kindly said a prayer and left.

The three of us sat quietly, each lost in our own thoughts. I can't say what Shaun and Emma had running through their minds, but I remember thinking, 'This is real, it's actually happening.' My best friend had gone and there was nothing I could do about it.

• • •

On the Saturday after Gina died, Shaun's old team Shepshed Rugby Football Club had a match scheduled. After clearing it with Shaun, they all wore something pink that day in memory of Gina. Shaun brought the boys along, and Shaun's dad was there along with other family members, all wearing something pink themselves. As the match was about to start the referee blew his whistle and both teams stood in a minute's silence as a tribute. The silence spoke volumes. In just a few seconds these big burly men would be charging round a pitch, aggressively tackling each other, shouting and swearing; yet here they were, standing stock still in reverential camaraderie, respecting Shaun's and the boys' grief and, perhaps, lost in their own thoughts of the wonderful lady they had lost.

Shaun was due to be at a motocross meeting on the following Sunday. He admitted that part of him still wanted to go, but that he felt guilty so we all told him that he should. Gina would have wanted him to and it would be good for the boys to get out of the house for a day. He and Gina had built up a good group of friends through motocross and we thought it would be helpful for Shaun to see them.

I wasn't able to go with them on the day as I had other commitments, but Shaun's brother David and his family were going to be there, so I knew there were people looking out for Shaun and the boys.

That night, when he got home, I spoke to Shaun on the phone. He was quite overwhelmed by the number of people that had come to him throughout the day to pass on their condolences and to say what a lovely woman Gina was. I asked him about his races and he said he wasn't sure how he had even managed to get round, as he had been blinded by tears. Every time he had come to the part of the track where Gina would usually stand, he automatically looked out for her. I told him that I knew she would be proud of him. I'm sure she was still there, cheering him on from the sidelines.

A couple of days later, Suzanne, the funeral director, rang while I was helping out at Shaun's house. I had brought Marco, Millie and Anni-Mae with me.

'Hello Jane,' she said softly. 'Could you please let Shaun know that Gina is home.'

I put my phone down, tears streaming down my face, and walked into the kitchen to tell Shaun. He simply nodded then disappeared upstairs. I didn't follow him, I stayed with the five children downstairs, and kept them busy making dinner. I knew that Shaun needed to be alone.

The following day Shaun said that he needed to think about what clothes he wanted to dress Gina in, now that she was 'home'. Again, he turned to me and Emma.

'I really don't know,' he said. 'Can you two decide, please?'

Emma and I took ourselves up to Gina and Shaun's bedroom. We sat on the edge of the bed looking at each other and said, almost in unison, 'Her wedding dress!' As we opened the wardrobe to find it, we both stopped in our tracks. Gina's clothes hung on the rails – not very neatly – waiting for her to pick out was she was going to wear for work the next day. Goodness knows how many pairs of shoes were stacked up in the bottom. Nothing had been moved since the day Gina stood in front of the wardrobe, making sense of the chaos. She had always joked that it wasn't chaotic in her eyes, as she knew exactly where everything was.

We wanted to make sure she looked her best for the big send-off. Emma and I found the pink gown that she had worn on the day that she and Shaun had renewed their wedding vows just over a year ago, then we slowly picked everything else from that day: shoes, jewellery, even the same underwear. I put her favourite perfume into the bag as well.

We knew that Gina had worn a shawl on that day but we couldn't find it anywhere. Suddenly,

Emma exclaimed, 'It was her something borrowed! She borrowed it from the lady that did her make-up on the day.' Our hearts sank. Neither of us knew her, but we needn't have worried. A couple of phone calls later we had the lady's name, address and telephone number. As soon as I explained who I was and why I was ringing, she asked me to come round and, when I arrived, she wrapped me in a hug, tears running down her face. Gina had only met her once but had obviously made a strong impression. She handed me the shawl, clean and folded neatly, and just said, 'Have it.' We now had the exact outfit that Gina had worn on that day, one of the most emotional days of her life.

Once we'd folded the clothes in a neat pile, we delivered the clothes to Suzanne and I told her, 'Don't forget to straighten her hair, will you?' Like me, Gina could never stand it if her hair hadn't been straightened. 'And please give her a squirt of perfume once she's dressed,' I added.

Suzanne phoned me a couple of hours later to ask if Gina had a brooch to hold the shawl in place. Shaun said that she didn't have one that he knew of, so Suzanne told us not to worry as she could discreetly use a safety pin.

A couple of days later I was going to see Gina in the chapel of rest. That morning I sat in my bedroom with my jewellery box on my knee. Somehow a safety pin for the shawl didn't feel right. I looked down at the cold metal that I was turning over and over in my hand – a silver brooch, not worth much but, to me, it was priceless. This little piece of costume jewellery had been given to me by my mum, who had passed away when I was 16. I treasured anything that she had given me, but most of all this brooch as it had originally been my grandma's. It was a bit battered and bent, with one of the little stones missing, but it was still beautiful. My mum had loved it and I knew she would have expected it to go to one of my daughters but, at the same time, I knew she wouldn't have been cross with me for giving to my best friend. In fact, I'd like to think that she would have been proud of me.

An hour or so later, I arrived at Shaun's house, showed him the brooch and asked if it would be all right to pin it to Gina's shawl.

He nodded his head. 'Of course, it's lovely,' he replied as he gently placed the brooch back in my hand.

On the way to visiting Gina, I remember feeling sick to the core. A number of people had said that they would come with me if I wished, but this was something I wanted to do alone. As I walked through the door of the funeral director's, I shook from head to toe. Suzanne greeted me warmly and guided me to a chair.

'Take as long as you need,' she said kindly.

Keri, Gina's sister, and her husband were already there. They went in before me and I could hear Keri crying through the door. After some time they came out and Keri offered to come back in with me. I shook my head, we said our goodbyes, and then it was my turn to enter the room. I knew what to expect as I had visited my mum, dad and grandmothers in chapels of rest, but that didn't make it any easier.

Suzanne opened the door to the little room and placed her hand gently on my arm as I walked in, then closed the door quietly behind me and left. It was just me and my best friend.

Gina looked like she was asleep. Her hair wasn't quite as she liked it but to me she was still perfect. I gently took her hand in mine and spoke to her between the waves of tears and emotions. I told her about the brooch and why it was so special and that I wanted her to have it now. I undid the clasp with shaky hands and pinned it in place on the shawl around Gina's shoulders. It was hard to let go of it when it was so special to me, but somehow I knew it was the right thing to do.

'Look after it for me,' I told her gently.

It was hard to believe that the last time she had worn these clothes she had been laughing and joking and as loud as ever, larger than life, appreciating every moment she spent with her family and friends. Now this horrible and unexpected turn of events had turned everything upside down and inside out. I knew that no matter how many times I asked why, I would never get an answer.

In the next four days before the funeral, I went to see Gina and spend time with her on a number of occasions. There were things I wanted to say to her, that I couldn't say to anyone else, and, in truth, I didn't like the idea of her being alone. On one occasion Emma was going to see her to say her own goodbyes. Like me, she wanted to go in alone but asked if I would wait in reception, just in case. I watched as she tentatively entered the room, following Suzanne, just as I had done, but within a few seconds Suzanne emerged and told me Emma was asking for me. As I walked in Emma was sobbing, so I put my arms around her and we both let our emotions flow freely. As we stood there crying uncontrollably, I suddenly realised just how strong we had both been for everyone else, keeping the depth of our devastation hidden from the kids, from Shaun and even from each other. But now we could let the sorrow out, united in our grief for our wonderful friend.

Amidst our care for Gina, the responsibilities of everyday life didn't stop. I had my own family to think of, but thankfully my sister Ann had really stepped into the breach and was helping to look after the children whenever she could. Anni-Mae's fifth birthday was on 20 October, two days before the funeral. Long before this all had happened, I had already booked a party for her. She was really looking forward to it. At one point, she reeled off a list of people who would be there, including Ashton, but then added, 'But Auntie Gina can't come because she lives on a twinkle star now.' I had to turn away because I was in bits.

Shaun was adamant I should go ahead with it, not wanting to spoil her big day and Ashton still wanted to attend, so Shaun agreed to bring him. 'He needs to be a normal five year old,' he insisted.

The party wasn't normal, though. Gina should have been there, the life and soul of the event as she always was. Ashton joined in with Anni-Mae and the other children as he normally would but Shaun stayed in the sidelines, clearly not in the mood for socialising and making small talk with other parents.

As I watched the children play, I remember feeling envious – but also glad – that they could forget the pain of what was happening, even if just for a short while.

• • •

All too soon, the day of the funeral arrived – 22 October 2010 – a day I was dreading. As the dawn broke I lay in bed, wide awake; I'm not sure that I had slept for even a few minutes all night. Instead I had spent the long restless hours trying to get my head around the fact that today I would be saying goodbye to a wonderful person and my best friend. She was just 34 years old and none of this made any sense. In the dark hours my thoughts turned to the day ahead. I fretted that I wouldn't be able to find the courage and strength to stand up at the front of the church and read the words that I had lovingly written, from the bottom of my heart, as a tribute to Gina. But I knew that today of all days I couldn't bear to let her down. It was the last thing I would be able to do for my friend.

Daylight crept through the curtains and I got up to get ready. In the bathroom, I found my shower had no hot water. I couldn't believe it. As I stood cursing, Marco tapped on the door. 'Are you okay, Mum?' he enquired, concern flooding his voice.

I explained about the shower. 'Just try to be calm,' he said, as he hugged me. But his caring gesture just set the tears flowing again.

'It's probably Auntie Gina playing silly buggers, eh?' I joked, through the sobs.

He nodded, with a sad smile on his lips that didn't reach his eyes.

Eventually, when we were all ready, I headed over to Shaun's house at Shepshed. I wanted to see Gina one last time so, after dropping the older kids off with my brother, and Anni-Mae with her grandparents, I went to the chapel of rest.

I had asked Marco and Millie if they wanted to see Gina to say goodbye, but they both said no. They had so many wonderful memories and wanted to remember her just how she was. Millie asked whether if she wrote a letter, would I give it to Auntie Gina for her. 'Of course,' I replied, and Marco decided to do the same. They gave me their letters in a sealed envelope so their words remain private, to this day. Anni-Mae drew a picture and wrote 'I Love You Jena' across it – she hadn't grasped the correct spelling for Gina and I didn't have the heart to tell her she had spelled it wrong. I took these tributes with me as I made my way to the chapel of rest.

It was so hard knowing that it was going to be the last time I could hold my friend's hand, or give her a kiss goodbye. I placed a small teddy, Anni-Mae's picture and an envelope with letters from myself and my children in the coffin with her, and then – somehow – I managed to say what I wanted to say to her, which will remain between the two of us. As I walked out of the room and closed the door, I felt a physical pain in my chest. I turned back, opened the door again and blew a kiss to Gina. I told her I loved her as much as a sister. 'Sleep tight, babe,' were the last words I whispered as the door slowly closed.

I had to sit in my car for a few minutes to compose myself before I headed round to the house, to Shaun and the boys. Emma arrived at exactly the same time as me and as we walked in, Shaun was putting down the phone cursing under his breath.

'This is not what I need today,' he spat out. We asked what the problem was.

'Bloody shower's not working,' he grumbled.

I had already told Emma about my shower problems and she and I exchanged a curious glance.

'Not yours as well,' I said, explaining the morning's mishaps to Shaun. He looked up at the sky and gently shook his head, 'Tut, tut, Gina,' he said gently under his breath. He was clearly thinking exactly what I had said to Marco earlier and I found it oddly comforting to believe that Gina was up to her usual mischievous tricks, and was watching somewhere, laughing. Within a few minutes Shaun's plumber friend was at the house and soon had the boiler running again.

Shaun wanted to be the last person to see Gina so he went to the chapel of rest to say his own goodbyes, while Emma and I got on with getting Lewis and Ashton ready. Lewis, like Marco and Millie, was given the choice to visit his mum in the chapel of rest, but he also said he would prefer not to. Shaun took some things to place in the coffin but I didn't ask what they were. I did not feel that it was any of my business; that was between Shaun, Lewis, Ashton and Gina.

The boys were very quiet as they got ready for the funeral, totally overwhelmed by what was happening. Shaun had ordered flowers arranged in the word MUM in lovely pinks and whites, and they each wrote their own cards to be placed on the flowers.

The boys had said they wanted to look their best when they said goodbye to Mummy so Shaun had got them matching ties for the funeral. They both put on black trousers and crisp white shirts, as well as the waistcoats they had worn when Gina and Shaun had renewed their vows. I crouched down to help them with their ties.

'You look very smart,' I told them. 'Your mum would be very, very proud.' I meant it: she certainly would be proud of them.

As the hearse and the funeral cars arrived, I felt sick to the bottom of my stomach. At the sight of that white box in the back of the hearse, it suddenly became real. Half of me was thinking, 'That's my friend in that box,' and the other half was saying, 'That's not her.' Conflicting emotions swirled around in my head as I fought to be strong for the boys.

Shaun had decided that he wanted to travel alone with Lewis and Ashton in one car, so Emma and I travelled in the second car with Gina's parents, and her sister Keri and her husband.

When we arrived at the church the pallbearers were waiting for us. They gently lifted the coffin up on to their shoulders and proceeded to the church doors, and as we entered the song playing inside became audible. 'Angels' by Robbie Williams echoed round the church as we walked down the aisle. I thought that it was incredibly fitting, as Gina was now an angel as far as I was concerned.

The church was absolutely packed with no space left, sitting or standing. There were even people standing outside because they just couldn't squeeze in. I noticed that all the friends Gina and Shaun had made at motocross were wearing their own personal race shirts, a spread of many different lovely colours in among the funereal blacks and greys that dominated the church. It somehow seemed right that Gina, who had been so colourful in life, should be celebrated in such a vibrant way. She would have loved it.

We took our seats as the song came to an end. I held Emma's hand in one hand and Lewis's in the other. Throughout the service Lewis and Ashton hardly took their eyes off their dad, unsure of what they should be doing, and copying his every move. I sat staring at the stark white coffin, not really hearing anything the vicar was saying, standing up automatically to sing the hymn we had chosen, 'All Things Bright and Beautiful'. 'How apt,' I remember thinking. 'Those two words describe Gina to a T.'

Gina's dad was brave enough to stand up and say a few words and then it was my turn. I took a deep breath as I stepped up to the front, trying to control the shaking in every part of my body, then I began to read the words that I had agonised over and rewritten several times, so desperately wanting to get them right.

This is what I said:

'When Shaun first asked me about speaking today I wasn't sure if I could do it, but I thought of Gina and how she would face each challenge that life threw at her head on, so I am going to try to draw strength from her.

'Gina had a lasting effect on people and you only have to look at Facebook, and at all the tributes and cards, to see that. The same words kept being repeated: "smile", "beautiful", "loving", "strong". AstraZeneca even flew their flags at half-mast as a sign of respect.

'Gina was very much a family person and treasured any time with her family; her mum, dad, sister Keri, Mike, and her niece and nephew, Rebecca and Nathan. Also with Shaun's family, who had become her own. If she wasn't with them they were never far from her thoughts.

'Shaun, her soulmate, and Lewis and Ashton were her world. She adored every minute spent with the three of them and would throw herself into anything the family shared, whether that be rugby, motocross or just family time at home.

'Sometimes things would knock her off her feet for a short time, then she would bounce back with some way of turning any situation into something positive, fundraising, pushing herself at the gym or just a good old party!

'Those who had Gina as a friend are the luckiest people in the world and I am so proud to be able to say that Gina was my best friend. I have many memories that I will always treasure and many experiences that we shared: being pregnant together, working together, Gina bouncing on the gym ball in my lounge when in labour with Ashton, to bouncing down Loughborough high street on a space hopper for her hen night, when she married Shaun for the second time.

'She wasn't afraid of anything that life threw at her and she met any challenge head on, with enthusiasm. She wasn't backwards in coming forward either. She had such a way with words and, boy, did you know if you were in the wrong! She wasn't afraid to tell you and you had no choice but to listen.

'Likewise, she wasn't afraid to tell you positive things either, make you feel better about yourself or just to simply tell you that she loved you.

'There is a saying that friends are the family you choose for yourself. How true. Gina was my sister of choice.

'I know that she will always watch over us and she would be so, so proud of Shaun and the boys, and be overwhelmed by the love and all the support from everyone.

'Shaun: you and the boys were the centre of her universe and she loved you far more than any words I could ever say. I promise you, Gina, that I will look after your three boys and always be there for them.

'We will all choose to remember Gina in our own way. Personally I will remember her ever-open arms and open heart, her beautiful smile and her amazing strength and friendship that will last forever.

'The angels are the lucky ones now! Sleep tight, beautiful lady, I will love and miss you always.'

A short way into my speech, I had a wobble and the tears began to flow. I couldn't get my words out, so Emma got out of her seat and came to stand next to me, putting her arm around me. She told me to take a deep breath and coaxed, 'Come on you can do it.' It spurred me on and I managed to get to the end. I just hoped that I had done Gina proud. I was still shaking and trying to control the emotion as I returned to my seat. Before I knew it the service was over and we filed out of the church as the Starship song played.

I couldn't bring myself to look at the faces of Shaun or the boys, frightened it would be too much. I couldn't crumble now.

They needed me now more than ever.

• • •

When we arrived at the cemetery I found myself walking next to Lewis and managed to pull him in for a hug. 'I'm so proud of you,' I whispered fiercely.

Ashton too came in for a cuddle and as I squeezed him tight, I told him that I loved him.

'Love you too, Auntie Jane,' he replied, so innocently.

It broke my heart to know that the one person in the world that they really wanted to hug them would never again be able to.

Shaun had made it very clear that he wanted Gina as near to home as possible so he had chosen a spot at the back of the cemetery, as close to home as the crow flies, next to the pathway and under the shade of a huge conifer tree. He had requested family and close friends only to this part of the day. As Gina was lowered into the ground, uncontrollable sobs racked through me. Yet at the same time I somehow felt numb, my mind reacting with disbelief to what my eyes told me I was witnessing.

I watched as Shaun kissed a rose and dropped it into the grave. Lewis took the lead from his dad and did the same, followed by Ashton, then a basket was taken round so that people could throw a handful of dirt into the grave. I took a handful. It felt cold, an empty gesture, throwing it into that big hole in the ground with my best friend at the bottom. It was too final.

Then that was it, it was all over. It was only now that I took in the huge number of floral tributes, in all colours, but mainly pink – Gina's favourite colour. They were so bright and beautiful. I had chosen a circle wreath, which had a special meaning to me and Gina. I had a Lovelinks bracelet, similar to a Pandora bracelet, and Gina had brought me a number of the circular beads to put on to it, always with the same message on the gift tag: 'A circle is never-ending, just like our friendship.' That is what I chose to write in return on the card on the wreath. And from that day, I have bought a circular wreath for special days, such as birthdays and anniversaries, and I always put the same message on before I put the flowers on her graveside.

When it was time to leave I turned to look at the place where my friend would forever rest, blowing her a final kiss. Emma and I walked back to the car hand in hand, silent, lost in our own thoughts and emotions, still reluctant to leave Gina alone, where she lay.

• • •

The silence continued on the way to the wake, which was to be held at the same pub where, just over a year before, we had celebrated Shaun and Gina's vow renewal. Walking in I was struck, once again, by the huge number of people present.

'Gina would love this,' I remember thinking.

The night seemed to go quickly with friends and family retelling their own stories about Gina, and there were lots of smiles and laughter amid the tears, just as Gina would have wanted. At the end of the night, Shaun's dad gave us all a lift back to Shaun's. I had agreed to stay the night to help with the boys, and if he wanted a drink at least he could have one.

Emma and I helped Ashton into his pyjamas, got him into bed and kissed him goodnight, then I went into Lewis's room to give him a hug and kiss goodnight. Shaun went upstairs after us and he was gone quite a while. What he said to those boys I will never know, and how the three of them got through the day so bravely was beyond belief.

The three of us – Shaun, Emma and I – sat talking until the early hours of the morning. The events leading up to the day and keeping it together at the funeral had kept Shaun's head above water but, at this point, the situation finally caught up with him as we sat down to talk. He was shaking from head to toe, and I will never be able to describe the pain in his eyes. Emma and I each held one of his hands in ours and, at that moment, he looked like a vulnerable little boy.

'I'm scared,' he finally said. 'I don't want to be alone.'

Yet again, tears rolled freely down my cheeks. I squeezed his hand. 'You will never be alone,' I told him. 'You have the boys and you have us, Emma and me!'

I had promised my friend just a few hours earlier that I would look after her three boys – and that was a promise I intended never to break.

CHAPTER 7

SOLDIERING ON

The days following the funeral were very hard. I, for one, felt bitter and angry. The world was carrying on as normal, with people complaining about being stuck in queues or having to go to work and other petty little niggles of everyday life. Didn't they know the tragedy that had struck the Hibberd family? The pain those two little boys had gone through, in losing their mother, was unbearable enough, but they still faced the prospect of losing their dad. When something so terrible happens it really does make you learn to appreciate what you have, and realise how small most 'problems' really are.

Shaun decided not to return to work for three very good reasons. First, he had been working as a lorry driver and starting at three or four in the morning, which was not something he could do now that he was solely responsible for Lewis and Ashton. Secondly, he needed to put his own health first more than ever and allow himself time to grieve. Finally, and most importantly, Lewis and Ashton needed him.

I continued to help wherever I could, sorting through the mountains of paperwork and forms that continually landed on the doormat, and making make telephone calls on his behalf, usually with him sitting at the side of me. He would often have to speak to the person on the other end to confirm he was happy for them to discuss his affairs with me, then let me get on with it. He was totally lost in how to manage all the admin and household papers, an area that Gina had always dealt with, so at least I felt I was of some practical help.

On one of these afternoons we were just finishing off a stack of paperwork and I was about to make Lewis and Ashton's packed lunch for the following day, when I said, 'I'll look after the boys when the time comes if you want me to?' He just smiled and nodded, and we carried on. We weren't to speak of it again for some time, but I was just glad that he knew that I was willing to be there for Lewis and Ashton.

Shaun's brother David and his partner Lisa felt the same as we did, that tragedy had taught them was that life was too short, so they decided that they would like to get married as soon as possible. They had set the date for 5 November 2010, just a couple of weeks after Gina's funeral. They wanted to keep it low key, with close family and friends only, but it was the end result that mattered. David invited Shaun to be his witness, which he happily accepted. After the ceremony, Lisa took her bouquet and laid it on Gina's grave, which I thought it was a lovely gesture and a touching tribute.

Sadly, I couldn't attend the ceremony as I couldn't get the day off, having already taken the two weeks following the accident, but I managed to get to the reception in the evening. Everyone looked wonderful and there was lots of laughter and smiles, but also a few tears. In the midst of the celebrations, it would suddenly come up and hit us again that Gina wasn't there, or I would find myself absent-mindedly looking round the pub for her, then suddenly remember I would never see that smiling face again.

Shaun still had hospital appointments for regular check-ups and I would accompany him so that he didn't have to go alone. The doctors were pleased with how he was doing and the most recent scan showed that the cancer had still not advanced any further so, every time, as we sat in the car on the way back from the hospital, I said a silent prayer: 'Please don't put this little family through any more.'

My sister Ann had been a huge support to me when Gina had died, despite being a twenty-four-hour carer for her husband Brian. I knew that if I knocked on the door she would make me a cuppa and listen as I talked or hold my hand as I cried. Now, as I still struggled to deal with my grief for Gina, I got a phone call to say that Brian had been taken into hospital. My sister and her family were beside themselves with worry.

Then the unthinkable happened. Brian passed away, just six weeks after Gina had been taken. I felt I needed to be strong again, this time for my sister, and my niece and nephews – but it turned out to be my big sister who was the strong one. Although crushed by her own loss and grief, she continued to be there for me whenever I needed her.

'It's what I need to do,' she said, one day. 'I'm your big sister, remember.'

In truth, we were there for each other.

• • •

After the horror of the past few weeks, life didn't hold much brightness. Even Christmas, by then just a few weeks away, couldn't lift my spirits. I missed Gina so much. No more planning Christmas shopping trips where we would spend too much money, giggling all the time and picking out presents for each other's children as well as our own. The excitement seemed to have died with Gina. I knew that it would be unfair on my kids to not at least try to make Christmas special for them though, and I encouraged Shaun to do the same for Lewis and Ashton – but I knew that it would not be easy for any of us. Gina had left a huge gap in all our lives that no amount of gifts would fill. I invited Shaun to join me and my family for Christmas day but he refused, saying he wanted it to just be him and his boys at home, which I understood completely.

Shaun battled on bravely, but he struggled with his grief, and every time he bought the boys a gift or some clothes he would ask himself, 'What would Gina think?' and, 'What would she have chosen?'

Gina and I had always agreed on a set amount of around £30 to spend on each other's children for Christmas and birthdays, and I didn't see why

I should do anything different this year. The only problem was that Gina wasn't there to shop with me, telling me what Lewis and Ashton had on their Christmas lists.

At just five, Ashton got as excited as any other child of that age does. As far as he was concerned, Santa was coming and he was looking forward to that. I was glad – a little boy should be excited at this special time of year, whatever awful blows the year has brought him. His age provided an innocence that I envied.

It was harder for Lewis. He was older, so part of the magic of Christmas was already gone for him, and knowing his mum wasn't going to be there, for the first time ever, made it especially hard for him. In the conversations I had with Lewis in the run up to the day, I encouraged him to enjoy Christmas as much as he could, telling him that's what his mum would have wanted, words I also repeated to Shaun. It was easy to say, but I was well aware it wouldn't be that easy in practice.

Somehow, we got through Christmas – and the New Year. To me, New Year's Eve had always been a very emotional time. My own mum and dad had always made a big thing about it and, since losing them, I had always felt a little lost around New

Year. I didn't expect this one to be any different and it wasn't, apart from the fact that people would now say, 'Gina died last year.' It somehow felt wrong saying that when, in fact, so little time had passed.

After Christmas, the boys went back to school and appeared to be doing well. Shaun turned out to be an excellent homemaker: the boys were clean and smart, the house spotless and there was always a hot meal on the table in the evening. Naturally, they had their bad days – I would have been worried if they hadn't – but on the whole they were doing incredibly well. I marvelled at the way they were all coping.

One day in January, Shaun sent me a text while I was at work asking him to call me as soon as I could. As always that set my alarm bells ringing, worrying if he was all right. The first moment I had to myself I called his number and frantically asked what was wrong.

'It's okay, don't panic, everything is fine,' he reassured me.

He went on to explain that a local charity, Wishes 4 Kids, had been in touch. It was a charity that usually helped children who had a life-limiting illness to fulfil a wish, but somehow they had heard about Lewis and Ashton's plight of losing their mum, and their dad being terminally ill, and wanted to grant them a wish. They had offered to send Shaun and the boys to Disneyland Paris for a long weekend, all expenses paid. Shaun was really touched and knew the boys would love it, so he was keen to go, but they told him that because of his condition he would have to take another adult, who would be classed as his 'carer'. He had asked the boys who they would like to go with them and they had said Auntie Emma or Auntie Jane. Shaun knew that I would feel awful about going to Disneyland without my own children, so he had asked Emma if she would accompany him, but she couldn't make it due to prior commitments, so that left me.

'That sounds lovely,' I told him. 'But I will need to think about it and talk to the kids, so I'll call you later.'

Marco and Millie were very grown up about it and told me that I should go, saying Lewis and Ashton deserved it. And Anni-Mae was due to be away at her dad's house that weekend so it wasn't a problem. I called Shaun that evening and told him that I would love to come with them. The charity called me the following day to confirm everything and just a few days later we were away.

My brother Mick came to stay with the kids and I felt sad and guilty saying goodbye to them, but guilt turned to pride when they told me, 'Just go. We will be fine, have fun!'

The charity had thought of everything. We had a car to the airport, transport laid on in Paris and a beautiful hotel. Ashton and Lewis were each given a card to hang around their neck, to let everyone who worked at the park know they were special so they didn't have to wait in queues for the rides. When there were any Disney characters around they made a beeline for the boys for a cuddle and a photograph, so they didn't have to wait to meet their favourite characters. Shaun had brought the boys autograph books and the characters all signed their name in it. It was particularly good for Ashton because, at five, he was at that age when he may have suspected that the person in front of him wasn't Buzz Lightyear, just someone dressed up, but at the same time he allowed himself to think that there was the chance that it *might* be Buzz Lightyear. Being older, Lewis was more interested in the rides, but the Disney side, the magical side, was still there for Ashton. He loved it and it gave us all some shared memories. I spent most of the trip behind the camera taking pictures of Shaun and the boys.

There were a number of times walking round the park I found that I was smiling to myself, remembering Gina – and I wasn't the only one.

On one evening, when we were on our way to eat, we saw a 'wishing well' style attraction, which consisted of a fake alligator in a pool of water, where you threw pennies in and made a wish. On our previous visit, Gina had commented on how lifelike it looked, but threw her penny in all the same – which activated the alligator to move and snap its jaws. Gina had screamed out loud, and jumped back with such force she fell straight on her bottom!

Being the great friend that I was, of course, I couldn't help her to her feet – because I was too busy laughing. In fact, we were all in stitches and she was soon giggling along with us, but it scared Marco, Millie and Lewis enough that they refused to throw their own pennies in.

On our return to the park we stumbled across the alligator, still in the same place, and even Lewis laughed. 'I remember that scaring Mum,' he said, with a half smile on his face. I couldn't believe that he could remember something that happened when he was so young.

Lots had changed since we had last been at the park a few years earlier, together as two families, but there were many things that hadn't changed at all and being back in the same place helped to make the memories flow easily.

And the memories were good, every single one of them.

• • •

Lewis's twelfth birthday was in February and Shaun asked him what he would like. I felt really proud of him when he said that what he would like to do was to go on holiday with his dad and Ashton so that he had a recent holiday to remember. Shaun booked a break in Tenerife for the three of them and Dick, a close family friend. During the week they were away I worried about the three of them non-stop, but I spoke to them on the telephone a couple of times and had regular texts from Shaun, so I knew they were well and having a great time. I was just pleased they could enjoy some quality time together.

Soon after their holiday Wishes 4 Kids held their annual fun day at Donington Park racetrack. The kids were allowed to choose to have a spin in ten of the many high-powered sports cars there. They had a go in everything from a Ferrari to an Ariel Atom, and Shaun and I got to have a go in a couple of them too. I was really pleased to be able to share these sorts of days with them, creating more memories for the boys to treasure forever.

• • •

One afternoon, not long after the event at the racetrack, I had just arrived home from work and sunk down into the sofa with a cup of tea, grabbing five minutes to myself before the school run, when my mobile buzzed at the side of me. It was Shaun.

'Trust you to ring just as I put my feet up,' I answered, laughing.

'Oh, sorry,' he said, in a flat tone.

'What's wrong? I asked. I knew that for Shaun to not come back with some witty comment, something must be on his mind.

'I have to choose the words for Gina's headstone,' he replied, with a catch in his voice. He knew the obvious – her name, date of birth, date of death, mum, wife – but he wanted a sentence that would be a fitting tribute. After much discussion I suggested 'Always remembered with a smile'. As I said to him, when you thought of Gina you couldn't help but smile, and every time you remembered her face, you always saw her big beautiful smile. Shaun was really pleased with that. I was just glad to have been of some help, and I did think it was very fitting.

But the final obstacle in our acceptance of Gina's death was still to come. The inquest into her death had been scheduled for mid-June 2011, and although we all knew it was going to be tough, it was something we needed to get through together, to find out the truth.

Even so, as the date got closer many of us were getting quite het up about it. No one, including Shaun, really talked about how we felt but everyone's patience was a little short, and I for one was quite irritable. Knowing only the sketchy details of the accident that I did, I had found myself having nightmares, imagining Gina trapped in the car with chaos surrounding her, shouting out for Shaun and her boys. Even though I had been told that her death would have been instantaneous, I couldn't stop thinking that she had been alone without any of her loved ones around her when she died. I never discussed it with anyone but I couldn't shake the images from my mind.

On the day of the inquest, I sat in the hearing room between Lisa and Shaun's other sister-in-law Jenny, holding a hand in each of mine. There were other members of Gina's family and close friends there too, along with representatives of the other driver. The atmosphere was extremely tense.

The court heard that the other driver's speed-
ometer was frozen on 79 mph, nearly 20 mph over
the speed limit, and that he had been swerving all
over the road. As he came over the brow of a hill
his car became airborne and landed in front of
Gina, who was driving in the other direction, like
'something dropping from the sky'. There was
nothing she could have done to avoid a collision;
the impact would have been immediate.

Then there were the medical experts who detailed
the injuries Gina had sustained. Horrific as it was to
listen to, they did state on a number of occasions that
Gina would not have been aware of her injuries. You
would expect that information to bring some comfort,
but given everything else we heard, for me and others
that I spoke to, it did nothing to help the nightmares.

It was incredibly difficult to hear all the minute
details of the events of that day, and to listen as the
witnesses gave their accounts of what had happened.
I had already read the witness statements as Shaun
had shown me his copy, but to hear it out loud was
a different matter altogether.

Mostly, I felt so incredibly angry. No matter what
anyone said or what verdict was given, this was all
wrong, so very wrong! I can't speak for others, but
for me it made me think 'what if' over and over

again. Gina had done nothing wrong, just been in the wrong place at the wrong time. If only she had hit the snooze button on her alarm clock that morning; if only she had left something at home and had to turn back to get it; if only…

Mairin Casey, the coroner, said: 'This is a situation, tragically, where one driver was driving far too quickly for the topography of the road. He lost control in an attempt to negotiate a left-hand bend and in so doing collided with Mrs Hibberd, who was driving quite normally in the opposite direction.'

At last they were ready to deliver the verdict: 'unlawful killing'. The other driver had been entirely to blame and Gina could have done nothing to prevent it. A whispered 'yes' resounded from people who were there for Gina. But it was a muted response. Yes, a verdict had been given, but did it make it any better? No! The only thing that could make any of this better was to have Gina back, and that wasn't going to happen.

About this time, I started to notice some changes in Shaun. Ever since he'd been diagnosed, I had occasionally seen him place a protective hand over his chest. I would ask if he was in pain and he would instantly snap back 'I'm fine' or 'It just aches a little.'

In the summer of 2011, however, I noticed it was getting more frequent and I could see in his expression that he was experiencing pain, not just an ache. He didn't want to expand on how he felt, though, and I didn't want to push him – knowing Shaun that would only make him clam up further. He was still having regular appointments at the hospital and I was confident they would be keeping a close eye on him.

For now all I could do was watch.

• • •

As the anniversary of Gina's death approached, mixed emotions surfaced all over again. In some ways it felt like only yesterday, yet at moments it seemed like forever since I heard her voice, gave her a hug or saw that beautiful smile.

On the actual day, we met up with family and friends for a drink to celebrate her life. I admit initially I had felt it was wrong to be getting together in the pub. Earlier in the day, I had visited the cemetery, alone, where I found that numerous bunches of flowers had been placed on the grave, including a huge bouquet from Shaun and the boys with a little card from each of the three of them saying how much they loved and missed her. I placed my flowers among the others, together with a picture Anni-Mae had drawn for her

Auntie Gina, and sat there for a while lost in my own thoughts, not really sure whether to attend later that evening or not.

In the end, I was glad that I decided to go. It was the sort of evening that Gina would have loved. The pub was once again packed and it was lovely to hear everyone telling their own little stories and memories of Gina. There were lots of tears that evening but also lots of smiles.

Although Shaun was often surrounded, I got a chance to speak to him on his own, briefly. I asked him how he had found the day and he shrugged his shoulders in a defeated way. 'We knew it was going to be hard,' he replied.

'She would be so proud of you and of them,' I said, nodding over to the boys.

He smiled then. 'I sure hope so.'

'I know so,' I insisted. Once again, I looked over at Lewis and Ashton, who were both talking easily with everyone in the room.

As the evening got later, Ashton got tired so he climbed on to my knee and snuggled his head into my shoulder. I hugged him close and carried on chatting with him curled in my lap. Sally, one of Shaun's good friends, spotted the two of us curled up together and came over.

'They are lucky to have you,' she said, nodding gently towards Ashton's sleepy head.

'They will always have me,' I replied.

• • •

That autumn, Shaun's health started to deteriorate. He wasn't breathless, but he was getting increasingly tired and struggled with pain in his left side. We would be sitting talking and he would suddenly gasp, clutching his side, then it would pass and he would carry on chatting.

Concerned, his consultant arranged a scan shortly before Christmas, and I went with him to get the results. We both sat almost silent in the waiting room. I was nervous, chewing my nails, waiting for Shaun's name to be called. I couldn't help thinking, 'What if it is bad news? How would Shaun take it? What about the boys?'

When they finally called his name I squeezed his hand in reassurance. It was the only comfort I could offer. I wanted to say, 'Don't worry, everything will be fine,' but it wouldn't mean a thing because I didn't believe it any more than he did.

The consultant met us with her usual light-hearted greeting and showed us Shaun's scan on the computer screen. She explained that the scan showed some small changes, but due to the pain he was now suffering it was likely that there were a number of microscopic changes that were taking place too.

As we left I remember thinking that we were no more in the picture than before we saw her. She said that nothing more was to be done at this stage, and Shaun was put on a cocktail of strong painkillers and told to come back in three months unless he noticed many more changes or there was anything that he was worried about. But I knew Shaun. He was a born stoic. For him to admit he was in pain, it had to be pretty bad. I also knew that unless it became unbearable, he wouldn't say if he felt worse. What if his own bravery turned out to be his worst enemy?

Whether it was the news from the hospital and his deteriorating health that made Shaun think about Lapland I will never know, but a couple of days later, over a cup of tea, he told me that he wanted to take the boys to meet Father Christmas. It was something that he and Gina had talked about a few times.

'Ah, that's lovely,' I smiled. 'They will love that.'

'So will you,' he replied, laughing. 'You're worse than the kids when it comes to Christmas!'

I looked at him, puzzled. 'I want us all to go, your children included,' he explained. 'That way, when

181

I'm no longer here, you will be able to talk to the boys about their memories of the holiday.'

I was really touched and couldn't wait to tell the kids. As expected, they were all really excited, especially Anni-Mae and Ashton, who still believed in Santa. We booked it with only a couple of weeks to go before departure, so getting ready for that as well as Christmas was hectic, but fun because we were looking forward to the trip so much.

Anni-Mae and Ashton each wrote a letter to Santa, but didn't post it.

'We don't need to,' they both exclaimed, their grins so wide they filled their cute little faces. 'We can give it to him when we see him!'

At last it was time to go. We got the kids up in the middle of the night to catch the flight, which added to the excitement. As we started the descent into Ivalo the view out of the aeroplane window was beautiful – snow covered everything. The magic began as soon as we walked down the steps of the aeroplane, where we were met by a couple of people in traditional costumes holding reindeer on a rope so that the children could pet them and have their photographs taken with them. Anni-Mae and Ashton were chattering away happily, trying to decide which reindeer they were and both agreeing on one thing: neither of them were Rudolf because they didn't have a red nose. Lewis and Millie were incredible – obviously too old to believe in Santa themselves, they did everything to make sure Ashton and Anni-Mae didn't pick up on it, chatting away about Santa and his reindeer and encouraging them to believe. Then we were whisked off to our hotel on the coach. The scenery was breathtaking. Every now and again you would see a couple of people dressed as elves sitting on top of a road sign waving to everyone. At the hotel we were kitted out in thermal hats, gloves, suits, socks and boots, which were absolutely essential with the temperature at minus seventeen degrees.

When we were muffled up and snug we went off to explore, Shaun and I pulling Anni-Mae and Ashton on a sledge behind us, and the older ones with a sledge under their arms. We braved the toboggan runs, the longest of which was a kilometre, then the kids had a number of goes on the smaller ones. Then we went back to the hotel, went for a swim in the pool, had dinner and the kids fell into bed exhausted.

'I don't feel well,' Shaun admitted, after dinner. 'I ache everywhere. I'm in pain and my throat is killing.'

I felt his forehead, he was red hot. I had brought plenty of medication with us so I dosed him up, hoping he was just coming down with a cold, or tonsillitis at worse. After a hot drink he decided to turn in for an early night and I went off to bed as well but, despite our exhausting day, sleep was a long time coming. My head crowded with worry as I remembered how sick Shaun had looked that evening.

The next day he didn't feel any better, but he put a brave face on, as usual, and we set off on the bus to a park. The kids knew that they were going to have a husky sleigh ride and a reindeer sleigh ride, but they didn't know that this is where they would get to see Santa.

We all had a great time, even Shaun, which was amazing considering how he was feeling. As the kids played in the snow a lady came over, discreetly took the Santa tickets from Shaun, then turned to the kids.

'I know where some of Santa's elves are playing,' she told them. 'Do you want to see them?'

Ashton and Anni-Mae took off so fast we virtually had to run to keep up with them. The lady led us to a beautiful forest and, as soon as we entered, elves jumped out from behind the trees, making the kids laugh out loud. We were settled into the sleigh drawn by four reindeer and off we went for our forest adventure. Every now and then we would see someone dressed as an elf sat up a tree, or behind a rock waving at us. Then there were reindeer and a sleigh on its side, with presents falling out of it. Ashton and Anni-Mae looked at each other, wide-eyed, and gasped, 'I think Santa might live near here.' As far as they were concerned, we were in the North Pole, not Lapland.

'What makes you think that?' I asked.

'Because there are presents and elves everywhere,' said Anni-Mae.

The sleigh ride carried on to a little log cabin, with Christmas lights twinkling in its windows and smoke rising from the chimney. It really did look like something from a fairy tale. The sleigh stopped and suddenly we were surrounded by elves, who lifted the children out and began to throw snowballs at me and Shaun, then encouraged the children to join in, which they did with undisguised glee, including Millie and Lewis who joined the fun happily! They were in their element.

Just then, the cabin door creaked open and another elf told the naughty elves off for throwing snowballs, then took the little ones' hands and led them to the cabin door. Inside a real open fire crackled under a fireplace lined with stockings, and there in the armchair next to it was Santa, in his big red suit with a snow-white beard that almost touched the floor. It really was magical. I looked at Ashton and Anni-Mae, their mouths wide open – then realised that my jaw had dropped too!

The two children went and sat on Santa's knee, each giving him their letter they had written and telling him they had been very, very good and what they would like for Christmas. We took some photos, and then we were off again on the sleigh heading back to the hotel.

The kids slept so well that night. I would have loved to have been privy to their dreams, but it doesn't take much to guess what was in them.

In my bed, however, I tossed and turned most of the night, and it's my guess that Shaun did the same. I had seen the sadness hidden behind his smile. I'm sure he was thinking the same as I was. I just couldn't help it. 'This could be his last Christmas with his wonderful boys...'

• • •

Back in the UK, we had a great Christmas Day, all things considered. We were a party of seven –

me with my children, and Shaun with Lewis and Ashton. We decided to spend the day at Shaun's as he and the boys wanted to be at home.

Shaun was adamant this was to be a Christmas to remember and he woke really early to put on a Santa costume that he had asked me to pick up for him. I couldn't help but laugh out loud when I saw him.

'Shhhh!' he whispered, putting a finger up to his mouth.

'What on earth is he up to?' I wondered.

Soon after he'd put the finishing touches to the outfit, we heard the younger ones excitedly waking up their older brothers and sisters.

'Don't say a word,' he warned, as he quickly ran into the lounge, shutting the door behind him. I gathered up the spare bedding from where Marco had slept downstairs and then headed upstairs where the five children were all sitting on one bed opening their stockings. I stood just outside the door for a few seconds, listening to their excited voices.

'Happy Christmas!' I shouted, bursting through the door. Anni-Mae and Ashton threw themselves into my arms and I gave them a big kiss and cuddle, then went to each of the older three in turn, giving each of them a Christmas kiss and a hug.

'Where's Daddy?' questioned Ashton.

'He's just cleaning his teeth, sweetheart,' I fibbed. 'Come on,' I added, rounding them up, 'let's go and see if Santa has left anything else besides your stockings.'

Anni-Mae and Ashton pushed and shoved to get out of the door first, with the older three close behind. We walked into the hallway and I put my hand on the lounge door handle.

'Shall we go and have a look?' Silly question – I already knew the answer – but they burst into the lounge and stopped dead in their tracks. Shaun was sitting in the chair in his full Santa suit, including hat and fluffy white beard. He had taken the throw from the sofa and covered himself up with it and he was pretending to be fast asleep. For once Anni-Mae and Ashton were speechless.

'Oh no,' I said, trying so hard to keep the smile from my lips. 'It looks like Santa has fallen asleep at our house, what are we going to do?'

They both shrugged their shoulders, standing stock still with gaping mouths, not taking their eyes off the sleeping Santa. Anni-Mae actually looked a bit scared. I turned around to look at the older three, who all had huge grins on their faces. Lewis shook his head, as though to say 'typical Dad'.

'Well, there are a lot of presents,' I pointed out.

'I think we should open them, but be very quiet because we don't want to wake Santa.'

The five off them went and sat on the sofa, huddled up together. I passed a present to each of them and they eagerly started to unwrap them. But as they started to tear at the paper, Shaun pretended to stir, stretched his arms and faked a huge yawn.

'Oh my, where am I?' he asked, in a low, deep voice.

'In Conway Drive, in Shepshed,' Anni-Mae and Ashton replied, almost in unison.

'Dear, dear me. I must have nodded off. It was that big mince pie and glass of beer you left me,' Shaun continued.

I was struggling to control the giggles building up inside me, and looking at Marco, Millie and Lewis, I could see they were too.

'Well, I had better give out your presents while I'm here, then I need to get the reindeer home and give Mrs Claus her present,' Shaun continued. He lifted a present up for each of the five of them and as he read out the tag on Ashton's, the excited little lad suddenly said, 'Auntie Jane go and get Daddy for me, he is not going to believe his eyes!'

That was too much. I couldn't hold the laugh in any more, nor could the older three, and our laughter set Shaun off. The secret was out. Once again, Anni-Mae and Ashton stood open-mouthed as Shaun removed the fake beard. Ashton ran straight to him. 'Oh Daddy!' he scolded, as he climbed on to his knee. Anni-Mae went over and gave Shaun a big hug.

'Merry Christmas everyone,' said Shaun, looking round the room at us all.

It was wonderful to see the five kids, laughing and playing together that day. Shaun and the male members of his family went down the pub, as was their Christmas tradition, and he took Marco and Lewis with him, leaving me to get on with the dinner, and the younger kids to play with their presents. Dinner was lovely (if I do say so myself!) and after the meal and into the evening, we all drank and ate too much, playing board games until the little ones could no longer keep their eyes open. As the three older children sat in the lounge watching a film, Shaun and I sat in the kitchen having a coffee.

'Thank you,' he said.

'What for?' I asked. 'I haven't done anything.'

'You have,' he replied. 'You have helped to make this Christmas amazing for us all – something I didn't think was possible without Gina.'

I was really touched. I swallowed hard, gave him

a hug and said, 'Thank you,' in return.

Then, to my surprise, he took my hand.

'This is probably my last Christmas,' he said sadly, looking at me simply.

I nodded, too choked to say anything.

'At least it has been one to remember,' he added.

He then filled up my glass, chinked his glass to the side of mine, and toasted, 'To family and to Gina.'

'To family and to Gina,' I replied.

Then we sat in silence. There was nothing more to say.

CHAPTER 8

PLANNING
FOR THE FUTURE

At the beginning of 2012, Shaun's condition grew steadily worse. The cocktail of painkillers that he was on didn't seem to take the pain away and the side effects were horrendous. He constantly felt sick, light-headed and dizzy, and he was barely able to keep his eyes open at times as he felt so drugged up. Because he was nauseous, he wasn't eating well and the weight started to drop off him.

One day he was due to see his consultant and it was all he could do to get dressed. I drove him to the hospital and helped him to walk inside, barely able to get him through the double doors. His skin looked grey and drawn and he was holding on the backs of the chairs to hold himself upright, not like

Shaun at all. The nurses all knew him as he had been attending so long and they could instantly see how ill he was, because this was way out of character for him. They were keen to get him lying down as soon as possible, so they led us to a small side room with a couch where Shaun could rest while waiting for his turn to see the consultant. Angela, Shaun's specialist nurse, came and sat with us and she too was shocked to see him looking so ill.

At last his consultant arrived and she was very sympathetic. She could see Shaun was suffering with the side effects and, to be honest, the drugs weren't having a lot of effect on the pain anyway so she said he needed to have an up-to-date scan as soon as possible. She also said that she was going to ask a pain specialist to come and see him. In the state he was in, Shaun didn't have the strength to argue.

The pain specialist arrived soon afterwards. She spoke to Shaun and gathered as much information as possible, having already been filled in on the situation by his consultant. But nothing could have prepared us for what she was about to say.

'I think you need to come and spend some time with us at LOROS,' she said, in a matter-of-fact voice. Shaun looked horrified and I was shocked.

LOROS is the local hospice – the Leicestershire and Rutland Hospice – and Shaun, like me, erroneously believed that a hospice was somewhere that you went to die. She saw the look of horror on both our faces and asked what was wrong. I told her what Shaun and I were thinking and she tried to reassure us, explaining that LOROS also provided palliative care, in other words, helped to control symptoms. Shaun didn't seem convinced but he felt too unwell to fight. When he looked at me, I saw the same look in his eyes that I had seen a number of times since Gina's death: fear. My heart went out to him but going to the hospice was for the best. I took his hand and tried to reason with him.

'It will only be for a couple of days,' I told him. 'You have to try something. You can't go on like this.'

'What about the boys?' he asked.

'Don't worry about them,' I reassured him. 'You know I will look after them.'

I promised I would stay at his house with all the kids and do school runs, packed lunches and so on before going to work. Eventually – albeit reluctantly – he agreed to go into the hospice. At that moment it took everything I had to be strong and look confident for Shaun. Inside, I felt a deep sense of dread and fear for the future, for Shaun and the boys.

The medical staff wanted to get an ambulance for Shaun, but he refused, 'I want to get there under my own steam,' he insisted. He later admitted that he felt everything was spiralling out of control and wanted to hold on to any independence that he could.

We spent a few more minutes with Angela, while the arrangements were made. Shaun perched on the edge of the couch, his head in his hands.

'What are you thinking?' she asked.

Shaun shrugged his shoulders, unable to speak.

'Come on, Shaun,' she coaxed. 'It's okay. You can tell me. What are you thinking?'

Shaun looked at Angela, then at me, then back to Angela. 'I think you are all giving up on me,' he said simply.

I had been as shocked as he when LOROS had been mentioned, so I was so upset by this presumption that I immediately got a bit defensive. 'How can you say that?' I asked tearfully.

'Not you, Jane,' he reassured me. 'But they obviously know something we don't,' he said, sweeping his hand around the department as though to indicate the doctors and nurses.

'Not at all,' Angela told him. 'But we need to get you feeling better than this so you can enjoy your time with the boys. If there was simply nothing at all that we could do for the cancer or the symptoms, I promise I would tell you.'

Shaun slowly nodded his head. He had a lot of trust and respect for Angela so I knew that her words meant a great deal.

We left the hospital and went straight to the hospice where we were met by the staff. As we walked through the front doors we were greeted warmly by the receptionist, who phoned through to the ward, then a nurse came down to meet us. She introduced herself to Shaun, then turned to me to shake my hand, saying, 'You must be Jane?' The hospital must have already explained who I was when they rang to book him in.

The nurse took us to the side room that was going to be Shaun's for the duration of his stay. I must admit, I was pleasantly surprised. I had imagined the hospice to be a sad morbid place, but that couldn't have been further from the truth. It was surprisingly welcoming, and not just Shaun's own room, which had an en suite and its own TV, but the whole of the hospice. The staff were lovely, friendly and helpful, and they did their best to make us both feel at ease.

The pain specialist came to see Shaun soon after we arrived to talk through the options with him. They mutually agreed which route he was going to try and, in no time, the wheels were in motion and the nurses were regularly bringing Shaun the new painkillers. I made sure he was settled and then left him to get some rest.

That afternoon, I was at Shaun's house when Lewis and Ashton came home from school. 'Hello, kids,' I said brightly as they came through the front door.

They smiled at me, putting their bags down on the kitchen table. 'Where's Dad?' asked Ashton.

I went over to them both and put what I hoped was a comforting smile on my face. 'Your dad has been feeling very sore lately,' I said, hoping that Ashton would understand my words. 'He's staying somewhere where they can help him with his pain. But don't worry, you can visit him and he'll soon be home.'

Both boys looked anxious.

'You know that I'm here for you both, don't you?' I said, reassuringly. 'And that you can always talk to me if you feel worried, or just want to blow off steam.'

'We know,' said Lewis quietly. I gave him a smile and, eventually, he smiled back.

I was so proud of them – both boys were so brave in the face of what must have been frightening news for them.

The following day Shaun had a scan so that the doctors could monitor the latest progress of the cancer and find out why his health had declined so rapidly, while he continued with the new painkilling treatment. Happily, within a week, Shaun's pain had improved, albeit only slightly, and he was discharged from the hospice.

But it wasn't yet time to go home. Instead, we went straight over to the hospital to get the scan results together. We were ushered into his consultant's room and sat nervously as Shaun's doctor closed the door and pulled up a chair to talk us through what they had found. Shaun's consultant was a very caring lady, but I could see in her face that something was wrong. It was bad news. The tumours in both of Shaun's lungs had multiplied and become bigger, and there were further tumours visible on his liver. After much discussion it was decided that Shaun would need to commence chemotherapy again, sooner rather than later.

Shaun simply nodded his head, stoically. 'I was expecting that,' he told her.

I don't know how he must have felt. His facial expressions gave nothing away. It was as though he was numb.

As we drove home from the hospital we both tried to be positive.

'Look how well you did last time on the chemotherapy,' I reminded him. Shaun nodded and gave a half-hearted smile, but there was fear in his eyes, mirroring my own feelings. Was this the beginning of the end?

We went home trying to be positive but within only a few days Shaun was back in the hospice as the pain had become unbearable, yet again. While he was there Simon, another specialist, came to see him and offered him a nerve block to try and numb the side where the tumours were causing the most pain. He was a wonderful man, very understanding and easy to talk to and Shaun liked him instantly. He had the procedure done, and the result was unbelievable. Shaun barely had any pain at all. He said that having no feeling in the left side of the chest was a weird sensation but he was more than happy to put up with that.

Simon also decided that he needed another scan so that was arranged for the following day, but neither of us thought too much about it. After all, it had only been three weeks since the last one. What could possibly have changed in that amount of time?

How wrong we were. In just three weeks the existing tumours had rapidly grown and, there were also metastases – or secondary tumours – in the pancreas and the adrenal glands in the abdomen. It was devastating news but, once more, I tried to be as optimistic as I could in front of Shaun. Lewis and Ashton were being stoical, brave boys, but I knew that the news that he needed more chemotherapy would be devastating to them.

On the strength of these results it was decided to start the chemotherapy straight away. Shaun was to have a different chemotherapy treatment to the one he had had two years earlier, but as before it would be six treatments, twenty-one days apart.

I offered to accompany him to the hospital on the day he was to receive the first lot of chemotherapy. Gina had always gone with him previously and I didn't want him to feel he had to face all this alone.

Shaun had the first dose of chemotherapy and his body's reaction was totally different from the first time around. By that evening, he was constantly vomiting and felt terrible. It affected him so much that I had to take a couple of days off work to care for him and the boys, as well as my own children and home. It was around nine days before he felt almost normal again, but the weight continued to drop off him, he was constantly tired and the pain seemed to be worsening day by day. He was again admitted to LOROS. This time they decided to try him on methadone, which meant he would need to be there for at least a week. Shaun was really unhappy about that but I managed to convince him that I could manage everything outside of the hospice and finally he agreed to stay.

By this time, Ashton and Lewis had sadly grown used to the fact that their dad sometimes needed to spend time in hospital. This time, I explained, it was going to be for a bit longer. I tried to put it simply to Ashton, saying that Daddy needed to have some 'special medicine', but Lewis later actually asked which hospital Dad was in. When I said 'LOROS', he looked confused.

'It's a hospice,' I explained, then I suddenly saw his face drop. I hadn't expected him to know what a hospice was. I quickly added that his dad was there so they could help him with his pain and that they had some very specialist doctors. He looked relieved. He must have thought it meant Shaun only had a few weeks to live.

'He will come home again, won't he?' he asked, full of concern. On this one point, at least, I could reassure him. Dad would be coming home; we just didn't know when.

During Shaun's stay at LOROS, I took Lewis and Ashton to visit a couple of times. Shaun was always so pleased to see them, and I think it must have been reassuring for Lewis and Ashton to see where their dad was, and what a nice room he had. The staff were really friendly, bringing them juice and biscuits, but it was always sad when it was time to leave. Ashton would often cry, while Lewis would put on a brave face, but I wouldn't be able to get two words out of him on the drive home.

While Shaun was in the hospice, my days were manic. I would get up around 5 a.m. every day to clean Shaun's house and put some washing on, then get the kids up and get them their breakfast, make sure they were washed and dressed in a clean school uniform and make packed lunches for the day. At 7.15 a.m., I would leave the house to take Ashton off to the childminder's, leaving Lewis behind to walk to the local high school. With Millie and Anni-Mae in the car, we would then drive the eleven or twelve miles to my house in Anstey, drop Anni-Mae at the walking bus to walk to school, ensure Millie had everything she needed for the day and see her off. Marco was now 18 and could sort himself out for work. After all that, I would then dash off to work myself. I usually finished around 1 p.m., so I would go straight to LOROS and spend an hour or so with Shaun, then back to my house to clean and wash before collecting Anni-Mae from school. Then I would grab a bit of shopping on my way back to Shaun's house, collecting Ashton from the childminder's en route, cook dinner, and help the kids with their homework before settling them down so that Shaun's dad could watch them while I went back to LOROS to see Shaun. After that it was back to Shaun's to do more chores, like ironing and washing. Eventually I'd fall into bed myself and start all over again the next day. But I wouldn't have had it any other way. I had promised Gina that I would look after her three boys and that was exactly what I was doing.

Although Shaun and I did our best to stay positive, we both knew that things were not looking good for him. We weren't stupid. One evening, when he was home from the hospice, we sat having a cuppa looking through some paperwork when Shaun simply said, 'Did you mean what you said?'

I looked up from the papers to find him looking straight at me. I knew what he was asking. He wanted me to look after the two remaining treasures in his life, his boys, when he was gone. I nodded, unable to speak for a moment because of the huge lump in my throat, but eventually I managed to say, 'Of course, I would be honoured.'

He went on, as though to make sure I understood. 'They're going to need so much attention,' he said. 'They have been through so much in their short lives.'

'I know,' I reassured him. 'I will love them as my own. I already do.'

Shaun took my hand in his. 'Promise me that you will never let them forget how much Gina and I loved them.'

Tears were rolling down my cheeks. 'I promise,' was all I could manage to say.

• • •

Shaun and I spoke a great deal over the next couple of days about me looking after the boys when he had gone. We agreed that I would only have the boys if Lewis, Marco, Millie, Ashton and Anni-Mae were all in agreement. It was hard to discuss the plans with Anni-Mae and Ashton as they were so little, and we were worried about how Ashton would cope. He had already been through so much in his little life, how could we tell him we were planning what would happen when his dad died too? He knew Shaun was ill, but he hadn't been told that Daddy was going to die. I had similar concerns about Anni-Mae and what she would be able to understand so, in the end, we decided to just ask them how they would feel about living together all the time. They both said 'yes' immediately and started jabbering away ten to the dozen, planning all the adventures they were going to have.

Shaun spoke to Lewis alone. I can't imagine how difficult that conversation must have been for both of them. He didn't tell me exactly what was said, but he reported the outcome – Lewis had said if he couldn't have his mum or dad, then he wanted me. I can't put into words how touched I was by that.

I sat down with Marco and Millie together, to ask them how they felt. I was incredibly proud of their reaction. A short way through my opening gambit, Marco said, 'Mum, before you go any further, you should have Lewis and Ashton.' Tears formed in my eyes as he continued, 'Lewis and Ashton are already like my brothers. I always expected that you would have them. It's what Auntie Gina would have wanted.'

Millie chipped in. 'They are so used to you being around,' she said. 'They know you love them and they are really going to need you.'

How did my two babies grow up so quick? So unselfish and loving. I couldn't have been prouder of the young man and lady they had become. They were willing to share me, their mum, with two more children and hadn't even needed to think about it. Their lives were going to change in so many ways but instead of putting themselves first, they were thinking of Gina and Shaun, Lewis and Ashton.

Shaun was relieved when I told him. We then spoke to them all together, agreeing that I would permanently move into Gina and Shaun's home. This was a really hard decision for me. I knew that Lewis and Ashton were going to be hurting beyond belief, and that being in their home with their memories all around them may be comforting in some ways, and certainly preferable to taking them away from their home and moving them into mine. On the other hand it meant that I would be uprooting Anni-Mae and Millie away from their home and their big brother, who wanted to stay at our house in Anstey. I understood that because his friends and his life were all there, but I still felt like I was abandoning him.

Typical Marco, he scolded me for my concerns. 'Mum, I'm 18 now and hopefully I will be a lot older before anything happens, so just do as you're told,' he insisted as he placed an arm around me. 'Anyway, someone has to look after our house till Lewis and Ashton are all grown up.'

I couldn't help but smile at that – Marco was no domestic god!

We had already decided that I would not sell my house, not just because my house is my children's future, but also because Shaun and Gina's house would eventually belong to Lewis and Ashton, so one day I will move back to Anstey. In the meantime, Marco would look after the house and contribute towards the bills, and he promised that he would visit often, even if it was just to drop off his washing!

Millie was at college studying for a diploma in animal management, as she had dreamed of being a vet since she was six. Luckily she could continue to go there while living in Shepshed, but I still felt guilty that I would be taking her away from her friends. Like her brother, she chastised me.

'I'm big enough to catch a bus when I want to,' she said. 'Just don't complain if I ask you for a lift!'

I hugged her tight. 'Thank you,' I whispered into her ear.

'Anyway, I could always stay with Marco the odd night if I want to,' she added.

Marco and I just looked at each other, raising our eyebrows.

From that day on, I cared for the boys the majority of the time. The chemotherapy continued with twenty-one days between each dose, and it got to the stage where Shaun was in bed for about fourteen of those days, too unwell to get up and go downstairs, let alone trying to do any normal activities. On a good day, I wouldn't need to go over, or I might pop over and make a lasagne for him to heat up later. But most days he couldn't even lift his head off the pillow. I would have to cradle his head and lift it to a glass of water to try to get him to take the array of medication that he was still on daily and I would need to be there to care for him.

But although Shaun was suffering greatly physically, his mind was still planning his boys' futures. Within three weeks of Shaun asking me to have the boys, and us speaking to the children, he decided he needed to have an extension built to make the house big enough for us all. He contacted a builder, whom he knew from the village, and he pulled out all the stops to help. The builder shuffled his jobs around, took on extra labour and then suggested a really good architect, with whom he was used to working.

The architect knew the family background and understood why Shaun wanted to get the building done immediately, so he pushed and pushed to get planning permission and it was granted really quickly. The original plan was to go from three bedrooms to five, so that each of the kids – barring Marco who was staying in Anstey – would have a bedroom. But Millie said, 'Mum, in two years' time I'm going to university. You don't need to have a room for me.' She decided she would share with Anni-Mae when she came home and Shaun altered the plans so that Lewis's room was massive, but could be divided into two rooms if Millie ever wanted to move in permanently.

Building work started in March and was completed in double quick time. The extension meant that Lewis and Ashton would not have to share again – as they did at the moment when I stayed over – unless they wanted to, which was a good thing because there is a big age gap between them. They were all very excited at choosing their own decor. Shaun even managed to complete most of the decorating himself, with a helping hand from me along the way. It was tough for him, and he could only manage the painting and papering on his better days, but he was determined to see the project through, and desperately wanted to make sure that we were all comfortable in the house when he was no longer there with us. Anni-Mae thought she was really special because she now had three bedrooms – one at our old house, one at 'Uncle Shaun's' and one at Daddy's.

In May, after much consideration and talking with Shaun, I decided to take some extended leave from work. Shaun really needed a full-time carer when he was at his worst and he needed frequent injections of strong painkillers. But he was just 39 years old and didn't want to have strangers coming in to tend to his every need. Besides which the boys also needed to be cared for when their dad was too ill and the constant rushing around was beginning to take its toll on me. We decided it would be better for everyone if I didn't have to work on top of everything else. My employers were incredibly understanding. They had seen that some days I was struggling and they knew that I was increasingly having to do more for Shaun and the boys, as well as look after my own children.

The pain Shaun was in fluctuated daily and he went back into LOROS numerous times so they could try different drugs and different procedures. Some helped a little and some didn't at all, others would make him hallucinate, which was scary for me to watch but must have been really frightening for Shaun. He was really struggling with the constant battle against this awful disease.

It seemed inevitable that, eventually, something would have to give. After four doses of chemotherapy out of the scheduled six, he turned to me one evening and said, 'I'm sorry.'

'What for?' I asked.

'I can't do this any more,' he admitted. 'The chemotherapy. I've had enough.'

My head was nodding but I couldn't get my brain around what he was saying. I must have looked like a nodding dog.

'You can't give up,' I said at last. 'That's not you.' My voice quivered as I said the words.

'I would rather have three months and be able to enjoy the time I have left, than six months constantly in bed, too poorly to even sit and have a meal with you all,' he insisted.

Although it was hard to take what he was saying, I understood his reasons for wanting to stop and, as always, I admired his bravery.

By now I was living at Shaun's on an almost permanent basis as he was spending more and more time in LOROS and was too ill to move when he was home. On his good days – which were still worse than most people's good days – he could get out of bed, he could look after the boys and even have a tickle fight. He would sit and have a meal with us or pop into town or to the cinema while the boys were at school. In fact, whenever possible, Shaun would get on his motocross bike and go out to race. The doctors told him not to, but Shaun would say, 'Take that away from me and I might as well die now.' Admittedly, he wasn't of the standard that he had been a year ago, but he loved it, so who were we to judge what made a dying man happy?

After Shaun had decided he wanted to cease the chemotherapy treatment we went to the hospital to speak to his consultant. She understood completely and felt that it probably wouldn't prolong his life that much anyway, given how aggressive the cancer had become. At least coming off the programme would solve the constant nausea and vomiting, and that would just leave the pain to try to get on top of.

Shaun and I continued to plan for the boys' futures. Sometimes he would just ask me to continue to bring them up with the same morals he and Gina had, but that wasn't going to be a problem. Gina and I had always been on the same wavelength when it came to raising children. Other times he would tell me to make sure I told them off when they needed it and not let them get away with things because they had lost their parents. But mainly he wanted reassurance that I would ensure they never forgot all the little details about their mum and dad.

The original arrangement had been that his brother David and his wife Lisa would have the boys, and he felt guilty about the change in plans. It wasn't that Shaun wanted them to have the boys any less than me, but since Gina's death they had had another beautiful baby boy, which meant they had three children under five. It wasn't fair to them to ask them to spread their attention even further on a full-time basis, and the boys would need a lot of attention. Also, I had been a constant presence in their lives for months now. The boys were used to my way of doing things and my routine, used to me nagging them to tidy up and making sure they were dressed in the morning. They had a horrible time coming up and we felt that as little change as possible might help them just a tiny bit.

When Shaun spoke to David and Lisa they completely understood. Yes, they were upset but promised Shaun that they would be a big part of the boys' lives, and they have been true to their word. They have been a rock to me and all five children, and been there for us every step of the way. I don't know what I would have done without them.

During our many chats about the future, we decided the school run back to Anstey for Anni-Mae was going to be out of the question. I didn't want Ashton to have to go to a childminder before school any more, so the obvious choice was for Anni-Mae to move to a primary school in Shepshed. Shaun and I went together to see the headmaster at Ashton's school and explained the situation. He said that although the school was full he would put in an application to have Anni-Mae transferred as soon as possible. By now we were into the autumn term and we agreed that we would wait until after the Christmas holidays, as she was already rehearsing for Christmas plays and looking forward to various festive events, so it was decided that she would make the change to the new school in January. Shaun said he really wanted to be around to see that she was happy and settled, which I thought was lovely. He was still worrying about his little princess when everything else around him was so uncertain.

I have received quite a bit of criticism for moving my children and causing upheaval in their lives to save Lewis and Ashton from any more changes, but I felt that this was a time when Lewis and Ashton needed stability. Any day now, they were going to be orphans, and they had lost both their mum and dad in a short space of time. I couldn't bear to think of dragging them away from their home, a place they could still feel close to their mum and dad with so many memories around every corner, and also away from their school and friends. I really believed that it would be too much. As a mum, of course I felt guilty knowing that Marco was going to be living on his own, though he reassured me daily it wasn't a problem. Millie would still be at the same college, and could visit her friends whenever she wanted. Anni-Mae was already used to staying at Shaun's and used to sharing me with Lewis and Ashton, so the only major change for her was moving to a different school. In fact, I was immensely proud of my children, who accepted all this change without one selfish comment and were kind enough to put other people before themselves. Not a bad quality to have in life!

With the decision now made about the boys' futures Shaun was keen to get everything settled and in place while he was still here so, although his will said that I would become the boys' legal guardian, he went to court to get an official ruling as well. Shaun deserved the peace of mind.

Things picked up for Shaun in some ways. Although he was constantly battling with pain he put a brave face on most of the time and he felt better without the chemo. He was managing to get on his motocross bike every now and then, so I decided that I would ride one weekend as a fundraiser for LOROS. The hospice had done so much for Shaun and I wanted to give something back. That was a big mistake – I loved it! I caught the bug and continue to ride to this day.

In late August 2012, Shaun decided that he wanted to go on holiday with the boys once again. He was realistic, knowing that this would be his last holiday, so he gave the boys the choice of where they wanted to go and they both said Tenerife, where they had been a couple of years earlier. We booked for a couple of weeks later, for all seven of us. Shaun insisted we deserved a holiday and, in truth, he never knew how he would be feeling when he woke up in a morning and needed someone there to take care of the boys if he wasn't able to. We had an amazing time, the kids all got on, and I even managed to teach Ashton and Anni-Mae to swim. Shaun struggled a lot in that week and couldn't even make it down to breakfast a couple of times, but he definitely made up for it when he was able.

One of the best days we had was when we went to the big water park, Siam Park, and Shaun got stuck in, whizzing down all the slides and playing in the waves with the kids. Some very special memories were created on that holiday. At the kids' disco I was amazed when Lewis and Millie got up to dance with Ashton and Anni-Mae, following the lead of the holiday reps as they did daft actions to all the songs, and laughing together. I caught it on video and to this day I tease them that I am going to put it on Facebook.

• • •

Before we went away, my sister Ann had been taken into hospital and we had been told it was nothing to worry about, just a flare up of her diverticulitis, a digestive disorder that she had long battled with. I was in touch with my family from Tenerife and there was no real change, which I was relieved to hear.

Four days after we got back, on the Tuesday morning, I got a phone call to say Ann had taken a turn for the worse. Panic surged through me. I travelled to the hospital with my brother and was told she had developed pneumonia. She was very poorly but they had started treatment, so we stayed a while then left her to rest and I then took Shaun to LOROS for yet another procedure. As we sat waiting for the consultant to come, my phone rang. It was my nephew, Neil.

'You need to come back,' he said, his voice wobbling with emotion. 'They are withdrawing her treatment.'

I couldn't believe what I was hearing; I had only left her a couple of hours ago but she hadn't responded to the antibiotics and now she was slipping away. Shaun told me not to worry about him, to just go, so once again I travelled back to the hospital with my brother. My sister died about half an hour later, with all of us at her side. She was just 61 years old. I was devastated.

Now it was Shaun's turn to support me. I rushed between Shaun and my family. Shaun kept telling me not to worry about him and the boys, but I did. Besides it kept me busy. Shaun came to Ann's house when my brothers, niece, nephews and I spoke to the vicar to arrange the funeral. He even accompanied the family to the chapel of rest when we went to see her. I remember feeling guilty at having him there, knowing that Shaun would be thinking that at some point in the not-too-distant future we would be arranging his funeral. But Shaun wouldn't hear any of it.

'You have done so much for me and the boys. Let me give something back,' he said when I told him how I felt. I didn't argue. I didn't have the strength.

On the morning of my sister's funeral, Shaun was due to be admitted to LOROS but he insisted on putting it off, saying that he wanted to support me on this emotional day. As I stood up in church to speak, I had a strange feeling. It was less than two years since I had done this for my best friend. Again, I had a wobble halfway through and couldn't get my words out. Shaun rose to his feet, ready to come and support me, but my brother, who was in one of the front rows, got there first.

'Come on,' he said, squeezing a hand around my waist. 'You can do it.' And I did. Another lady that I hoped was proud of me for what I said that day.

After the funeral we went back to the social club where my sister often met with her friends and played bingo and, just as I had after Gina's death, I felt like I was on the outside looking in. Shaun had to leave early to go to LOROS but I couldn't have got through the service without his support. There were no words that could thank him enough.

CHAPTER 9

THE DRUGS DON'T WORK

The death of my sister hit me hard. She was quite a bit older than me and, after losing both parents when I was 16, we had become incredibly close. My grief for her made me relive parts of my grief for Gina all over again, reawakening emotions that had never really gone away but had been bubbling under the surface. I missed them both so much and at times was overwhelmed by grief. Two of the ladies that I would turn to when I was struggling with anything had gone. I was so angry with life in general. It was so unfair, there was no rhyme or reason that I could find that made it any easier to deal with.

Occasionally, when I could feel the anger bubbling uncontrollably to the surface, I would go for a walk alone to somewhere open and deserted and scream, but more often than not it surfaced as angry tears that would burn my face as they slid down my cheeks. I would make up any excuse to leave a room so that Shaun, the boys or my own children didn't have to see me cry. At times I felt angry with my mum and dad, Ann and even Gina. How could they have left me? I knew it was irrational and the overwhelming guilt I felt when I had thoughts like this took my breath away.

To make matters worse, Shaun's health continued on a steady decline. It got to the stage where none of the painkillers or procedures were helping with his pain any more and the side effects of the drugs were almost as bad as the pain. He was constantly dizzy and nauseous, there were times when he could hardly keep his eyes open and would fall asleep over his dinner or cup of tea. He had to inject himself with painkillers at home, which helped a little bit, but he could only have them every eight hours and they wore off long before that so he would sit watching the clock, wishing time away so that he could have another dose and another short respite from the pain. Yet again he was admitted to LOROS where, after lots of discussions, they decided to give him some radiotherapy. They made it very clear that this was in no way a treatment for the cancer, it was purely palliative, a treatment of the symptoms. They were confident that it would help with some of the pain. Shaun was not only in pain all down his left side, where the pain had always been, but he had constant abdominal pain and excruciating pain in his back. He couldn't lie flat because of the pain and constantly had an electrical heat pad and hot water bottle behind him so that he could sit without being doubled up. He would have the hot water bottle so hot that it started to burn his skin, but he didn't care. He had got to the stage where nothing mattered to him any more, the pain was controlling him and he hated it.

He was more than willing to give the radiotherapy a go. As far as he was concerned he had nothing to lose and he would have tried anything. He was fed up with walking around like a zombie, full of drugs that were doing nothing to help him.

It was easy for anyone, including the kids, to see that things were getting a lot worse for Shaun. He would try to have the usual banter with Lewis and Ashton, and chat about their school day and their friends, but it was becoming increasingly difficult. Either he was too tired and falling asleep mid-conversation due to the drugs, or in so much pain that his face would contort as he tried to ride it out.

He would sometimes take himself off to his room when it got too much. He felt so guilty that the boys should see him like that and he didn't want the way he was to be their lasting memory of him.

The consultant decided to do another CT scan and bone scan prior to the radiotherapy to fully reassess things. Shaun had never had a bone scan before but really wasn't fazed by that. Being prodded and poked had sadly become the norm.

But I knew that deep down Shaun was frightened. He knew that things were not good so whenever I could get family or friends to help with the children I would stay at LOROS, sleeping in a chair at the side of his bed. Nobody deserved to feel that they were alone while going through this hell!

Shaun's consultant came to see us on the day following the bone scan in mid-October. Just when you thought that nothing could get worse – it did. He explained that the scan had shown even more tumours. As well as all the organs the cancer already occupied, it had also spread to his ribs and his spine, which explained the back pain. I was taken aback. I couldn't help but think that earlier this year Shaun had been astounding everyone with how well he had been doing, and now this. The consultant went on to say that they were still happy to go ahead with the radiotherapy, but made it very clear that things were not good. I wasn't brave enough to hold my feelings in check this time and Shaun and I cried together for a long time after the consultant left the room.

'Will I see Christmas?' Shaun asked, eventually. I stood motionless unable to speak, and finally I managed to shrug my shoulders.

'I really don't know,' was all I could say.

'Then I need you to speak to the consultant again for me, I need to know everything.' he begged.

Reluctantly I agreed, I went and spoke to the nurse who promised as soon as the consultant was back on the ward, she would let me know. Shaun's good friend Phil arrived half an hour or so later; Shaun and Phil had a great relationship, and the constant banter would always lift Shaun's spirits. As Phil shook his hand and sat down, Shaun casually announced, 'I've had it, mate. My time's nearly up.'

Phil looked over at me and it was obvious that he didn't know whether to cry or laugh. Shaun was constantly teasing him with phrases like, 'You buy the pints. I'm dying, remember.' It was just Shaun's wicked sense of humour, which Phil shared. But Shaun went on to put him in the picture about everything that the consultant had said. As he spoke there was a rap on the door, the consultant popped his head round and, looking from Shaun to me, enquired, 'I understand you wish to see me?'

I nodded and rose out of my chair. He looked over to Shaun and asked if he was happy to let him discuss things alone with me.

Shaun nodded in agreement. 'I want you to tell her everything,' he confirmed.

I was dreading the conversation. The consultant took me into a quiet little relatives' room. I couldn't help but think of the hundreds of people that would have sat in that room before me, after being told that their loved ones had passed away.

'How can I help?' he asked calmly.

I wasn't so calm, my heart was racing, my hands were sweating and the lump in my throat was making me feel like I could barely breathe, let alone speak. The consultant waited patiently until I had composed myself, then I repeated the conversation I had had with Shaun.

'How long?' I asked.

'A few months, maybe,' he replied.

'How many months?' I said in quick response. 'Six? Eight?'

The consultant shook his head slowly. 'Maybe it would be better if we said weeks rather than months. I'm only talking two or three months.'

I stared at him, open-mouthed, totally taken aback and unable to take this news in. 'He wants to know if he will be here for Christmas,' I told him at last.

The consultant sat looking thoughtful for a moment. 'I really can't answer that,' he said.

I gulped down my tears. Christmas was only ten weeks away!

'We can't put an exact time on things,' he explained. 'But there is just as much chance that he will make it for Christmas as there is that he won't.'

None of this was what I had expected him to say. In truth, I had hoped that he would chastise me for being silly and say, 'Goodness me, there will be months yet!' But it wasn't to be. The consultant commended Shaun for his bravery and said that he felt that, in light of the kind of person that Shaun was and the way his disease had behaved, Shaun wouldn't deteriorate much more, that he had reached his worst and would just slip away when the time came.

I tried to let his words sink in. I couldn't believe that Shaun, who had come so far and been so brave, wouldn't be able to beat this. I thought back to the first time we had arrived at LOROS. We had passed a room where an old man lay in bed, and the poor soul was just skin and bones, he looked so ill. Shaun had dropped his head after we walked past, then he took my hand and said, 'Please don't let me ever get like that.'

I had tried to keep things light-hearted by saying, 'You won't ever be like that, look at the size of you!' Shaun was a big man, not fat in any way but very muscular. He had always looked after himself and he played rugby for over 20 years so he was very well built. Over the last few months, however, he had shrunk from around seventeen stone to twevle, but he had lost it all in proportion. If you didn't know him you would look at him and think he was as fit as a fiddle – but to those who knew him the change was drastic. Shaun was unhappy with the weight loss so it provided a small glimmer of comfort when the consultant had said he didn't think that he would deteriorate much more.

The consultant left the room and a nurse came in with a cup of tea for me. 'Take as long as you need,' she said comfortingly. The next thing I knew the tea was stone cold and I was sitting on my own in that little room, so lost in my thoughts I hadn't even heard her leave.

I returned to Shaun's room where, perhaps surprisingly, Shaun and Phil were in full banter mode, laughing and joking. It was good to see.

I joined in with the conversation as much as I could, then Phil stood and said it was time for him to go.

'Pub's open,' he joked.

'Have a pint for me,' Shaun said, shaking his hand.

'Don't worry,' said Phil, 'I intend to have a belly full for you.' He was smiling but the worry and sadness was evident in his face. He walked round to the side of the bed where I sat. I stood to give him a hug and kiss, and as he left he put his arms around me and simply whispered, 'Thank you.' I was so moved, I just nodded, too frightened to speak in case I broke down, and Shaun needed me to be strong. As Phil walked out of the door he turned and said to us both, 'If you need anything you only have to ask.' We knew he meant it.

I was so tense after Phil left, that every muscle in my body was aching. I sat rigid, waiting for Shaun to ask me what the consultant had said – but he never did. Instead, he said, 'I know it's going to be hard, but will you please do something for me?'

'Anything,' I said, though I was already worried about what he might ask.

'I want you to go and tell those that need to know that time is limited now,' he said.

229

Shaun's policy had always been to be open and honest, and not to hide anything, so I was not surprised that he wanted them to know. I wasn't sure how I was going to have the strength to do what he asked, but I had to try. I checked who he wanted me to speak to, then I left, planting a kiss on his forehead and promising him I would be back once I had done what he had asked, and fed and showered the kids and got them into bed.

It was rush hour and the traffic was horrendous, although for the first time ever I was glad. It gave me a chance to try and make sense of the day so far and practise in my head the conversations I was going to have to have with Shaun's family. As soon as I felt composed enough to cope, I went to see Shaun's mum and dad. As I walked down the drive, Shaun's mum saw me and cheerily waved hello through the window. I must confess I pretended that I hadn't seen her, as I knew I would not be able to make a smile reach my lips. I knocked on the door and walked in, and she cheerily called from the lounge, 'In here, my duck.' I took a deep breath and opened the lounge door.

'Goodness me, you look exhausted,' she said. 'Go put the kettle on, Mick,' she instructed Shaun's dad.

'Wait,' I stopped him. 'I need to speak to you both.' I sank to my knees in front of Shaun's mum's chair, took her hand in mine and proceeded to tell her what the consultant had said.

They were heartbroken. I remember Shaun's mum saying with a sob, 'I brought him into this world. He shouldn't be leaving it before me.'

As she spoke I looked at them both and thought to myself that no one should ever have to lose a child, no matter what age they are. They had treated Gina as a daughter and had taken her death hard, but now the death of their son was becoming a reality too.

Afterwards, I went to see David and Lisa, and David agreed he would be with me when I spoke to Lewis – the conversation I was dreading the most. I really didn't know how he would react and thought that having another male present, especially his uncle to whom he was close, would help in some way. I also called Rich, Shaun's best friend from childhood. I felt so bad having to tell him on the phone, but as he lived in Holland I didn't have a choice. Each person I told was devastated.

Shaun and I had decided not to speak to Ashton, as we felt he was too young to understand what was happening, but Lewis had to be told and I couldn't put it off any longer. David arrived and I asked Lewis to come and sit with us as we needed to talk to him.

I took a deep breath as I started to talk Lewis through the day's events and before I had even finished that poor young boy was beside himself. Part of me had imagined he would be the way he usually was – stoical, just like his dad, putting on a brave face. But he crumpled. He just kept saying, 'I knew this would happen. What have I done to deserve this?'

I tried my best to comfort him, telling him how much his dad loved him and encouraging him to make the most of the time that they had left.

'I will, I will,' he repeated over and over again.

I held Lewis as he cried, David and I both telling him we would always be there for him. I'm not sure how much of the conversation sunk in apart from the fact that his dad only had a very limited time left to live.

I can honestly say that that day was one of the worst days of my life.

• • •

Later that evening, I made dinner and helped Ashton and Anni-Mae with their homework. I was on autopilot. My brain was on overload, there was too much happening to make sense of it all. With the young ones in bed, Shaun's dad came and sat with the older ones for me so that I could go back to LOROS and to Shaun.

When I arrived I gently opened the door to his room and peeped my head round to find Shaun asleep. 'I hope he has nice dreams,' I thought, creeping in carefully so as not to wake him. I had been there for twenty minutes or so when his eyes fluttered open. Seeing me there beside him, he reached out for my hand.

'It's been a shit day, eh?' he said bluntly.

I nodded in silent agreement. He then asked me to go through what had happened, who I had spoken to, who I had seen in the few hours since I left him. I told him everything. Shaun believed that honesty was the best policy and he expected that in return. He wouldn't have thanked me for smoothing over the details. He would have known I was lying and would not have appreciated that.

Shaun listened silently as I described the reactions of his family and friends, and relayed their messages to him. When I told him about Lewis, sobs racked through his body, uncontrollable and seemingly never-ending. I held him as he cried, tears flowing freely from myself as well. I had only seen Shaun cry a couple of times before, and certainly never twice in one day. The emotion had just been too much for him to control. We spent the rest of that evening in silence. There were no words to say.

Eventually Shaun fell asleep, I sat beside his bed a while longer, watching his chest rise and fall, and thought I would go and fetch a drink and get some fresh air. But as I went to stand his eyes flew open.

'Don't leave me,' he begged. I reassured him I was just going for a pit stop – a drink and to use the bathroom. He looked relieved.

'Thank you so much,' he said again.

'You really don't need to thank me,' I returned.

I meant it, too. Without Gina here to take care of him, he needed my support. I wasn't about to abandon him.

I had promised her.

CHAPTER 10

SLIPPING AWAY

The day following that dreadful news, Shaun seemed to be in amazingly high spirits. He was chatting, laughing and joking when I went for my usual visit at the hospice. I had been there about an hour when he decided he felt up to having a shower.

'I stink!' he said bluntly.

I laughed and said, 'Well, I was going to tell you but didn't want to upset you.'

'Cheeky cow,' he replied, laughing.

'I am going to fetch some tea and biscuits,' I teased him. 'If you're a good boy and have a wash, I might let you have some too.'

He promptly struck the two-fingered 'V' sign at me. But as I was about to leave his room, he came and stood in front of me, put his arms around me and put his head on my shoulder which, if I'm honest, I believe was so that he didn't have to make eye contact with me.

'So,' he began, 'am I going to see Christmas?'

This was the moment I had been dreading. He wanted to know exactly what was said during my conversation with his consultant. I couldn't lie, that isn't me, so I answered truthfully. 'He says there is as much chance that you will, as there is that you won't,' I braced myself, not knowing what to expect.

'Well, that's good enough for me,' he said, surprisingly chirpily.

'What do you mean?' I asked, slightly confused.

'Simple,' he replied. 'If there is a chance that I will be here we need to start planning. Believe me, I intend to make it a Christmas that no one forgets!'

I knew that he meant it, that he would pull out all the stops to make his last Christmas as special as possible. I'm sure I saw a glimmer of a spark in his eyes that had been missing for far too long.

He disappeared into the bathroom and I walked round to the cafe area, speechless. I was in awe of that man and truly hoped that I was at least half the person that he was. He knew he only had a matter of weeks to live, yet here he was still putting others first. Yes, he wanted to be able to enjoy Christmas, but more than anything he wanted it to be a Christmas that everyone else would remember.

By the time I got back with the tray of tea and biscuits, Shaun was out of the shower and was lying on the bed dozing. I quietly placed the tray down trying not to wake him – no such luck. From behind me, he said, 'I hope you've got chocolate biscuits.'

I laughed, swung round and said, 'Well seeing as you no longer smell like a wet dog you can have some,' playfully tossing him a packet of biscuits. I went to sit down and take a slurp of my tea, when I heard, 'Hold on, hold on. You need to get a pen and paper first.'

I went to speak, to ask him what it was for, but as I opened my mouth he stopped me.

'Please,' he said, pulling his best puppy-dog face at me. I dutifully went off to get some paper and a pen from one of the nurses, and when I came back in I asked, in mock subservience, 'Can I sit down now, sir?' He just gave me a mischievous grin and nodded.

We drank our tea and ate our biscuits before I asked, 'So what are we writing? My Christmas list? If so this paper is not big enough!'

'There's plenty of room to write an apple, an orange and a piece of coal,' he joked. I promptly stuck my tongue out at him and he laughed, but then his face clouded over and turned more serious. 'There are things we need to plan,' he said, sadly.

'Oh Shaun, we don't have to do this now,' I said, a lump rapidly forming in my throat.

'I want to,' he insisted. 'I need to. Once I know this is done I can get on with making the most of the time I have left.'

Who was I to argue?

We spent the next two hours planning Shaun's funeral. Obviously he wanted to be buried in the same plot as Gina. He chose a white coffin, exactly the same as hers, and the pallbearers he would like to carry him. A couple of them would be the same people who had carried Gina, others were friends he had chosen because of the amazing support and help they had given him since Gina's death. He wasn't religious so didn't want to choose any hymns, but chose three songs to be played during the service. We decided that the order of service and the memorial cards would be identical to the ones we had both chosen for Gina. He picked out the clothes that he wanted, saying he didn't want the traditional suit and tie that he believed people would normally be dressed in. 'I want something comfortable, that I look at my best in,' he explained, choosing his jeans and one of his favourite red T-shirts, the shoes he wanted, which were his red Vans to match the red T-shirt, and even which aftershave he wanted to wear. He asked me to make sure that they didn't shave him – Shaun hadn't had a close shave since his hair grew back following the first round of chemotherapy, preferring the designer stubble, as he put it. He told me that he wanted me to be the first person to see him in the chapel of rest – he even joked that if he looked rough I wasn't allowed to let anyone else see him – and he wanted me to be the last person 'before they hammer in the nails'.

Shaun also explained that he wanted two cars to follow the hearse, the first for me and the five children, the second to carry his mum and dad, and his brothers David and Andy, with their partners. He asked me if I would choose the words to be placed on his headstone, after discussing it with his boys, obviously. He even stated that he wanted his wake at The Bottom Railway, the local pub. His exact words were, 'Make sure everybody has a bloody good piss-up.'

We talked about the personal things that he owned and who he wanted to have them, or things that people were to be given. He asked me to make sure that I kept his and Gina's remaining things safe, and give them to the boys when they were old enough.

He had a will in place, but the only items specifically covered were his and Gina's wedding rings. There were other items that had a great deal of sentimental, rather than monetary, value and it was important to Shaun that these items went to the right people, people that he had chosen and he knew Gina would have chosen if she had had the chance. I promised him I would ensure every one of his wishes was carried out.

Again, he seemed relieved that the boys were going to live with me and that it was now legally set in stone.

While this conversation felt like one of the hardest I have ever had in my life, Shaun was very matter of fact about it all. I tried to mirror that for myself but it was so tough. The man in front of me was the bravest I had ever met. He had dealt with losing his beloved Gina with so much pride and strength, and now here he was facing up to his own death in the same way.

I had no idea he had planned this so thoroughly and in so much detail, and I was touched. He really did want everything sorted. I think he knew the less I had to deal with the more time and attention I would be able to give all the kids, especially the two most precious to him, his wonderful boys.

After I had written everything down he read through it a couple of times to make sure he hadn't missed anything, then he called for the doctor and asked him to witness the document. The consultant signed beneath Shaun's name, and Shaun thanked him and shook his hand before he left the room. Then he turned to me, placed the folded-up piece of paper into my hand, folded my hand around it and said, 'This is yours now, you need to look after it until it's needed.' It was horrible knowing that he was really saying 'put it somewhere safe till I die'.

He never mentioned the letter, wish list, whatever you want to call it, again. I hid it away and there it would remain until the dreaded day when I would have to get it out and read it again.

• • •

Shaun came out of LOROS on 12 October 2012. It's a date that sticks in my mind because it was the second anniversary of Gina's death and he was feeling really guilty, because he hadn't been discharged in time to visit her grave. I told him not to worry, I had bought flowers and taken them to the cemetery with the boys. He didn't have to tell me he was grateful, I knew he was. I also knew that he would still beat himself up because he hadn't managed to get to the cemetery himself.

The boys would often accompany me or Shaun to the cemetery, Ashton more often than Lewis who, being older, would sometimes go off on his bike to visit the grave and preferred to be on his own. Ashton, on the other hand, was almost excited, running off to the grave as soon as he got out of the car.

On this day I explained it was a special day as Mummy had now been an angel for two years. I encouraged Ashton to talk to Mummy and he did, telling her what he had been doing at school and what I had cooked him for his tea. I unwrapped the pink flowers that I had brought and he enjoyed helping to place them in the vases.

'Mummy will be well happy with them, they are her favourite colour,' he remarked.

I nodded, smiling. 'They sure are, buddy, they smell nice too.'

Ashton bent down and sniffed one of the flowers. 'Mmm, they do smell nice,' he agreed. 'Just like my mummy did.'

I had to turn away and take a deep breath; what he was saying was so sweet and innocent. I didn't want him to see that I was struggling with the day and could barely hold the tears back. I wanted him to feel comfortable at the cemetery, not just today but on future visits as well.

As we stood to leave, Ashton said, 'Bye bye, Mummy.'

I kissed my fingers then touched her name on the headstone, as I always did when I visited her grave. I started walking away but, realising Ashton wasn't on my heels, I turned to look for him. I caught him copying what I had just done, kissing his own fingers and brushing them across the gravestone. Since that day he has done that every time we visit the cemetery. A special way to say goodbye.

• • •

Later that evening Shaun said, 'You always manage to think of everything.'

'Yeah I know,' I gloated. 'That's because I'm a woman and I can multitask.'

He grinned. 'You are great. You know that, don't you?'

He was being serious, but I just said lightly, 'I couldn't agree more, Mr Hibberd.' In truth, I couldn't say what I wanted to, that he was the great one, a true inspiration. Shaun and the boys were so happy to be reunited at home that I didn't want to spoil the moment by getting emotional.

Within a few days, Shaun was back at the hospital for the dose of radiotherapy that they hoped would ease his pain. They had warned him that he could feel very sick and tired, but for once he didn't seem to get the side effects. He was no more tired than usual and didn't feel sick at all. In fact, he seemed better than he had been for a good few months. I kept crossing my fingers, scared that it was too good to be true.

Soon after the treatment, he even managed to get out on his new motocross bike. He had bought himself the latest model, a brand-new KTM, and had got personal decals – the stickers that decorate the plastics of a motocross bike – with his mate Phil's company logo on. He also bought himself new kit: matching motocross shirt and trousers, even managing to get gloves and goggles to match so that he was all coordinated. He was as proud as he could be and it was great to see him out on track. He didn't ride particularly well as the effort was too much for him, but boy, did he enjoy it and it was uplifting to see him laughing and joking with his motocross buddies.

With his love of the sport reignited he asked if I would accompany him to the International Dirt Bike Show on Thursday 1 November and I eagerly agreed. I now loved the sport too, though I was torn between motocross and road racing, having taken part in both. The kids couldn't come because they were at school but we had a really fun day. Shaun treated himself to a couple of new accessories, and enjoyed stopping and chatting to people that we bumped into throughout the day. He was worn out by the time we got home but the next day he decided he wanted a trip to Ikea, so who was I to argue? A daytrip out shopping with the added bonus of meatballs for lunch. Perfect!

On the Saturday, Shaun decided that he wanted to get some fireworks and sparklers in for the kids. Rich and his partner Nat were over from Holland and arranged to join us for the evening. Lewis and Ashton were looking forward to seeing them because they had known Rich all their lives and loved Nat too.

That evening was freezing cold but that didn't stop us enjoying it. I made sure the kids were wrapped up warm in hats, scarves and gloves, and I put on plenty of layers myself. We must have looked like we were going on an expedition to the North Pole, not just out into the garden. Shaun and Rich took control of the fireworks, setting them off to the cheers of the kids. Shaun was laughing and joking throughout, even prancing about in the garden when one of the fireworks fell over and the sparks shot across the lawn rather than up in the air.

Ashton was laughing out loud at his dad. He grabbed Shaun's hand and said, 'Come and stand out of the way with me where it's safe, Daddy!'

We oohed and ahed as the fireworks lit up the night sky, with the odd scream as the bangers went soaring into the air.

'Do you think Mummy can see the fireworks?' Ashton asked, taking hold of my hand, craning his neck backwards as he peered upwards at the stars.

'I'm sure she can, buddy,' I replied, ruffling his hair.

The kids loved making shapes in the air with the sparklers, or writing their names, and they thoroughly enjoyed the whole evening.

With the family fireworks over and sparklers finished, Lewis headed out to a fireworks display for his friend's birthday with a cheery, 'See ya later, Dad!' Meanwhile, I got the two little ones ready for bed. Kitted out in his pyjamas, Ashton crawled on to his dad's lap for a big kiss and hug.

'Love ya, son,' Shaun said, giving him a squeeze.

'Love you too, Daddy,' Ashton replied brightly.

I took Anni-Mae and Ashton upstairs and tucked them in, their little cheeks glowing from the cold. They were asleep in minutes. I came back downstairs and put the kettle on, making us all a hot drink and within a few minutes Shaun was also asleep. I didn't think anything of it, and neither did Rich and Nat. We were all used to Shaun being sleepy for so many months now. The three of us sat chatting, laughing at Shaun's not-so-gentle snoring coming from the sofa.

He woke as they were leaving, we said our goodbyes and arranged to see them the following day. I helped Shaun with the injection that he was still using regularly for the pain and then got into bed myself.

I woke up a few hours later, aware that Shaun had got up to use the bathroom and I instinctively checked on him as I always did, enquiring if he was okay. All he said was, 'That's really taken it out of me.'

'Just get back into bed,' I told him. 'You need your sleep.'

Less than an hour later I was woken by Shaun for a second time, this time calling out to me. As soon as I walked into his bedroom, I knew something was wrong. He grabbed out for my hand.

'I can't breathe,' he almost spat out.

He was semi-upright and was gasping for breath. I could hear the rattles coming from his chest.

'I'm ringing for an ambulance,' I told him. He was too ill to argue.

I called 999 and explained the situation, then phoned Shaun's dad, Mick. I told him what was happening and he arrived just before the paramedics so he waited outside on the pavement to direct him up to Shaun's bedroom. By now Shaun was red hot and his breathing had become more difficult. The paramedic listened to Shaun's chest with a stethoscope – not that he needed one, as the bubbling sound that came from his chest was incredibly loud.

'His lungs are full of fluid,' he confirmed. He set up a nebuliser and asked me to hold the mask over Shaun's face while he called for an emergency ambulance. Several times, Shaun tried to push the mask away.

'Just let me keep it there,' I begged. 'It's to help you.'

It felt like an age before the ambulance arrived, although I have since been told it was only about twelve minutes, but by this time, Shaun couldn't even stand. They tried hard to get him on to his feet but to no avail. Shaun was very confused and frightened, but they each took an arm and held him upright so that I could pull some jogging bottoms on him, then they strapped him into a chair and took him down the stairs and into the back of the ambulance. Mick said I should go with him to the hospital, and he would stay and mind the kids. As the ambulance pulled away from the house, the two crew members looked at each other and said, 'Blues and twos,' meaning they would have the blue lights flashing and use the sirens if they came across any traffic, and that confirmed my worst nightmare: things were bad. En route to the hospital a tube was inserted into Shaun's hand and a drip attached to it. An oxygen mask was placed across his face, and he finally closed his eyes and relaxed back into the pillow. Then they asked me to confirm Shaun's details, his medical history, and wrote down the long list of his medications that I recited to them.

After being rushed into Accident and Emergency, Shaun was taken to a booth and the doctor came immediately. As he was too poorly to move, they X-rayed him where he lay and began giving him antibiotics for an infection.

As the doctor explained the treatment, all I heard was the word I had been dreading: 'pneumonia'. I'm not usually a pessimist but the first thing I did was think of my sister, who had died just over six weeks earlier from that very thing. My heart was in my mouth as he continued. I could see his lips moving but I was only hearing certain words – 'serious', 'life-threatening', 'very poorly'.

Shaun's pneumonia had attacked his right lung, his good lung – or at least the better of the two – and had produced a lot of fluid. His temperature was dangerously high which, in turn, had caused his confusion.

As they fussed around him, I quickly nipped outside to phone Shaun's dad and brother with an update, and then I phoned my own brothers. Then I just sat at the side of the bed, waiting for some kind of response. I was terrified. Part of me didn't want to be there at that moment, but I also knew that there was no way I was going to leave.

As dawn broke, Shaun appeared to come round a little bit, but he was still disorientated. 'I need to spit,' he muttered. 'My mouth tastes horrible.'

I grabbed a handful of tissues and placed them in front of his mouth, I wiped away when he had finished and went to place the tissues into the bin. What I saw horrified me – the tissues were full of bright red blood. Panicking, I ran out through the curtains and grabbed the doctor looking after Shaun.

'He said he wanted to spit,' I explained. 'But look!'

I continued holding out the tissues so he could see the crimson contents. He didn't look at all alarmed, just nodded and placed a hand on my shoulder reassuringly as though to say 'I'm not surprised'. I returned to the cubicle where Shaun lay on the trolley.

'What's wrong with me?' he asked, barely able to manage more than a whisper.

'You have pneumonia,' I replied, again reminding myself that Shaun wouldn't thank me for not telling him the truth. 'They have started antibiotics to fight the infection,' I explained, hoping that I sounded more positive than I felt.

A short while later we were moved to a ward. I called Rich and Nat and they agreed to go and stay at Shaun's house with the children to give Shaun's dad a break.

'Don't worry about anything,' Rich reassured me. 'We will have them as long as necessary.'

Shaun was very sleepy but would wake for ten minutes or so now and again, usually to complain: the nurses were too noisy, the tea was horrible, etc. I took this as a positive sign, he was being his usual self. They continued with a regime of antibiotics, paracetamol to keep his temperature down and painkillers. I kept family and friends updated as much as possible but my phone was still constantly vibrating in my pocket.

Shortly after lunch, Shaun's friend Phil arrived to visit. Shaun was the best I'd seen him all day, even managing a bit of the usual banter he had with Phil.

'Take her home will you,' he said, cocking his head towards me. 'She's doing my head in.'

He winked as he said it, of course, to make sure I wasn't offended. Even so, with my car at home, having come in the ambulance, I decided to travel back with Phil to freshen up, see the kids, and get Shaun some clean clothes and toiletries. We had left in such a rush in the early hours of that morning that I hadn't thought to pack a bag.

I promised Shaun that I would be no more than a couple of hours, and started to gather my belongings and put my coat on. Phil stood from his chair and bent over the bed to give Shaun a hug and I remember thinking, 'Ah, bless.' As Phil stood, Shaun reached out for his hand and said three words, 'Love ya, buddy.' Phil placed his free hand over Shaun's hand and said, 'Love ya too, mate.'

I had to turn away. It sounded like a last goodbye. I didn't want to think like that but I couldn't help it, the emotion it stirred up inside me was crushing.

At the house, Rich and Nat were desperate for an update. I explained that it was pneumonia and that it was really just a waiting game. Then I had to tell Lewis what was going on.

He was up in his room. I knocked on his door then tentatively opened it, not sure even then of what I was going to say.

'How is he?' he asked, before I was even fully in the room.

Hard as it was I knew I had to be honest.

'He is very ill, mate,' I said.

Lewis dropped his head into his hands. I sat down next to him to try to explain what they had said at the hospital, but it was all a bit too much for Lewis to take in, despite me trying to explain it as clearly and simply as I could.

I put my arms around him and he sobbed softly for a few minutes. I promised him that when I got home, no matter what time it was, I would wake him up and keep him updated.

Lewis didn't want to go to the hospital to see his dad, as he was frightened of seeing him so ill. I couldn't help but agree with him. I found it frightening enough myself and it looked like things were only going to get worse.

True to my word, just a couple of hours later I was

pulling into the car park and getting Shaun's bag out of my boot. As I walked on to the ward, the sister came to greet me, 'We have put Shaun in a side room,' she explained. 'That way you can stay as long as you want.' I didn't really think anything of it apart from, 'At least he will have a TV now.' I walked through the door of the room and I instantly felt differently. The air was heavy and the mood was sombre.

'Hey, I'm back to irritate you again,' I said, trying to sound light-hearted. Shaun just gave me a funny look. I sat in the chair next to him. 'What is it,' I questioned, already dreading the answer.

He replied simply, 'They have put me in here to die.'

I took his hand and tried to reassure him, but all I could say was, 'No, it's so someone can stay with you,' but I wasn't convincing myself, so I'm sure it wasn't convincing to Shaun either.

For the next couple of hours we were both pretty much silent, and Shaun drifted in and out of sleep. At one point I got myself into a state as I realised the date, 4 November, was the anniversary of my dad passing away. 'Please God,' I silently prayed. 'Don't take someone else away from me.'

In the early evening Shaun again appeared to come round a bit. He was more chatty, asking after the boys, my children, was I okay? Had I let everyone know he was in hospital? He even asked for the TV to be put on. He never mentioned his illness again and nor did I. We didn't need to because it was at the forefront of my mind at all times, as I'm sure it was his. The only kind of reference to it was when he quietly said, 'Sorry.' I knew he meant for what he had said when I had first walked into the side room, but I just playfully nudged him and told him to shut up.

By 10 p.m. Shaun was sleeping soundly. I knew that the children would be fine and be getting spoiled by Rich and Nat, so I decided to stay at the hospital. I wouldn't have slept if I had gone home anyway, so I settled myself into the little camp bed the staff had brought in for me. I didn't expect to sleep well but I was exhausted and fell into a restless sleep not long after Shaun. I woke a few times through the night, but at 5 a.m. I was startled by sudden movements from Shaun. I scrambled out of the covers.

'It's okay Shaun, I'm here,' I said. 'What's wrong?'

I didn't get a reply so I went towards the bed. Shaun was thrashing about and didn't seem to hear anything I was saying. He was wet through with sweat and his breath was coming in rapid, sharp gasps. Breathless with panic, I rang the call bell for help and the nurse was with me almost immediately, but she couldn't seem to calm him down either. There was a doctor present on the ward, so he assessed Shaun and a decision was made to give him some morphine in case he was in pain, hoping it would also have the possible side effect of calming him. He had the injection and initially it appeared to have worked, but the lull was short-lived and Shaun was soon thrashing about again. It was heartbreaking to see and watching it was proving a bit too much for me to bear. With nobody to turn to, I crumpled into the arms of a nurse, unable to control my emotion.

Once they had got Shaun settled again she asked if there was anyone I would like to call. I looked her straight in the eyes and asked if she was telling me that I should call his family. She put her hands protectively on my shoulders and said that I should call his nearest and dearest. Her words knocked the wind out of me. They didn't expect Shaun to get through this.

After I had called Shaun's brother David, his parents, my brothers and Phil, the doctor took me in a private room and explained that the antibiotics did not appear to be treating the infection as quickly as they had hoped, his lungs were still full of fluid and although he was having these 'episodes of thrashing around', for the most part he was unresponsive. He suggested that they sedate Shaun and I was horrified. I couldn't count the times he had said to me, 'Don't let them make me into a zombie.' I was so torn. I wanted to respect Shaun's wishes to the last, yet I couldn't bear to see him in the state he was. Occasionally he would open his eyes but they looked full of fear and I'm not sure he knew we were there. We didn't know if he was in pain, but one thing I knew for sure was that he was frightened.

The doctor also went on to say that if Shaun's heart stopped they would not attempt to resuscitate him. My head was spinning. How, in just thirty-six hours, had he gone from enjoying fireworks with family and friends to being, to put it bluntly, on his deathbed?

Within a couple of hours my brother Mick, David and Lisa, and Phil were at Shaun's bedside with me. I had described how he was on the phone, but I could see in the faces of each and every one of them the pain when they saw him for themselves. I couldn't leave the room without Shaun appearing to panic and start thrashing about, trying to pull his drip lines out and the oxygen mask off his face.

If I went to the bathroom, I could hear those with him saying, 'It's okay, she will be back in a minute,' trying to reassure him. I would spend ages talking to him, holding his hand, stroking his forehead. I couldn't bear for him to think he was alone.

One time, as I reached his bedside after briefly leaving the room, he grabbed my jumper and pulled me to him, enveloping me in a big bear hug, I couldn't help sobbing as I placed my arms around him and held him. All of a sudden, though, he lashed out, catching me with a right hook. I know it wasn't intentional but it still knocked me backwards with such force that I stumbled into the open bathroom door behind me. Composing myself, I stepped forward to his side again rubbing my cheek.

'I'll let you have that one, Hibberd,' I said, just in case he could hear me. I didn't want him to feel bad.

During one of his worst episodes it took me, David, Lisa, Phil, three or four nurses, two doctors plus a couple of students to restrain him in order to stop him hurting himself. He gripped my brother's hand so hard that he was bleeding.

Occasionally, Shaun's eyes would open inter-mittently and he would seem to look at one person then another, then another, the fear in his eyes blatantly obvious for all to see. The doctor turned to me and asked if I thought he was in pain and, angry with the situation, I said, 'Maybe he doesn't like being the freak show!'

That may have been a bit unfair but at least the students who were standing round his bed not doing anything useful, discreetly left the room. Eventually Shaun calmed down again and the doctor again asked us about sedating him. I looked over at David for guidance. 'I promised him,' I sobbed. 'But I can't do this any more, I can't bear to see him like this.'

David and I agreed together to let the medical staff sedate him. I felt so guilty, but what if he was aware of what was going on? What if that was what triggered the fear in his eyes? Nobody deserved that.

Rich and Nat came to visit Shaun before he was sedated and were shocked by what they saw. I had taken the decision, after discussing it with the family, not to bring Lewis and Ashton to see their dad. I was struggling to cope with what I was seeing and I couldn't put them through that. I knew it would be a memory that would stay with them forever, and it wouldn't have been a good one.

Eventually people had to leave: Nat and Rich to get back to the children, David and Lisa to sort their own young family out. My brother Mick stayed on. His son, Stephen, works in theatres in the hospital so he said he was waiting to give him a lift home but in truth, I think he was reluctant to leave me. When my nephew finished work he came up to the ward to see Shaun, then they did have to go. I have never felt so alone. I sat constantly talking to Shaun. I didn't know if he could hear me but I needed to be sure that if he could, he would know that I was still with him.

At eight o'clock that evening Mick re-appeared at the door of the room, knocking gently.

'I'm not leaving you on your own,' he said. 'I want to stay.'

I nodded sadly, it meant so much to me and I know it would have done to Shaun too. He was closely followed by David and Lisa.

'David is staying with you tonight,' said Lisa, embracing me. I nodded in agreement, the ache in my chest stopping me from speaking. I checked that David was happy for my brother to stay too, which of course he was, and the staff arranged another temporary bed to be put in the relatives' room so that David and Mick could try to take it in turns to get some sleep. I still had the camp bed next to Shaun's.

A short while after they had arrived we noticed that Shaun's breathing had changed to loud rattling, gasping breaths. The nurse called for the doctor who examined him and informed us that Shaun was starting to overload, which meant that the fluid in his lungs was increasing. He said that if he didn't improve soon they would take the decision to withdraw treatment. This was too much to hear. I rudely barged past the nurse. Lisa tried to reach for me but I headed straight out the door, and then allowed myself to fall to pieces.

Lisa followed me out and held me for goodness' knows how long until the tears subsided, then I pulled myself together. Shaun needed us now. We had to be strong and stand united for him. Lisa had to leave for the children and left me sitting on Shaun's right side holding his hand, David on his left holding his hand and Mick sitting at the foot of his bed. We were sitting quietly, chatting about nothing in particular, when suddenly the room went eerily quiet. There was no sound coming from Shaun. He had stopped breathing.

Instinctively I shook his shoulders. 'Shaun, Shaun, wake up, please wake up.' I had pressed the nurse call button and they came immediately.

'I'm sorry,' said a nurse gently. 'He has gone.'

All three of us were sobbing. Shaun had slipped away at the age of just 40 years old. This terrible cruel disease had claimed another life, and Lewis and Ashton were orphans.

CHAPTER 11

TOO MANY GOODBYES

The three of us – David, Mick and I – sat for a while with Shaun. We continued to speak to him. David had broken the news to Lisa and, as he was so stricken with grief and unable to speak to his parents, Lisa agreed to speak to them on his behalf. David managed to speak to his brother Andy, who was away on holiday. I told other family and friends, and I called home to speak to Nat and Rich, who were with the kids; Ashton was fast asleep in bed but Lewis was still awake in his bedroom watching TV. I asked that they waited and let me tell him when I got home.

It wasn't long before the news started to spread and texts from people wanting to pass on their condolences started flooding in. I suddenly panicked. What if Lewis, Marco or Millie saw a comment on Facebook before I had had a chance to tell them the news myself? I quickly rang Rich and Nat and explained my fears. They agreed to tell Lewis, just in case, and the three of us made the decision that it was time to leave together.

A nurse had been in to take some of Shaun's tubes out and, as she removed them, she said, 'Sorry, Shaun,' which I found touching. She advised us to take all his personal belongings home with us, including jewellery, so I took his leather bracelet from his wrist and passed it to David, telling him, 'Look after this till he can have it back.' I hated removing his yellow Livestrong wristband, which he had worn since the day we had got them, just a few weeks after he had been diagnosed, as had Gina and other family and friends. He had never removed it before. I placed it over my own wrist where my own wristband sat, then removed his necklace, telling him that he could have it back soon.

The three of us each said our own personal goodbye. I asked Shaun to give Gina and my mum, dad and sister a hug from me and, once again, I promised to look after his boys. I tried to tell myself not to look back as we left the room, but

I couldn't help myself, neither could David. We both broke down yet again as we softly closed the door behind us.

From the hospital Mick drove us straight to my house where Marco and Millie were with a friend. Marco heard Mick's car pull up and was already at the door before I put my key in the lock. He took one look at our faces and he instantly knew. He threw his arms around me and pulled me close to him. I managed to mumble, 'He's gone, Marco.'

'I know, Mum, I know,' he sobbed.

I'm not used to seeing Marco cry and the raw emotion in those tears was heart wrenching. I went upstairs to Millie, who was sitting on the end of her bed, already crying. She had heard us downstairs and had guessed what I had come to tell her. I wrapped my arms around her and she didn't hold back, letting the sobs come.

'At least he isn't in pain any more,' she said, eventually. 'He is back with Auntie Gina.' I nodded in agreement. Millie followed me downstairs and went straight over to hug David, who had been a close family friend since Gina's death.

By the time I had gathered up the few belongings that I needed, Marco and Millie had disappeared, so I went upstairs to look for them. Millie was curled up in bed and Marco was sitting on the bed next to her holding her hand. Seeing them looking out for each other in such a caring way set me off again. I knew they loved each other but I was used to them arguing like cat and dog, and I hadn't seen them look this close since Gina had died. I asked them to come back to Shepshed with me but they said they'd rather stay at home. They knew that I would have to talk to Lewis and Ashton and, in truth, I don't think they felt strong enough to face them. I hated leaving them after telling them something so awful, but I knew my friend would look after them and I had to respect their wishes. Most of all they had each other.

There were lots more tears and hugs as I kissed them both goodnight.

'Promise me you will call me if you need me,' I said. 'I will come straight back to collect you.'

They nodded and I gave them one last, lingering hug before we headed back to Shepshed. Mick drove us to David and Lisa's house, where I shared a tearful hug with Lisa, but I was eager to get home to Lewis who, by now, would have been told the news by Rich and Nat.

As we pulled up outside, I sat for a minute to compose myself, then went in to Rich and Nat and asked where Lewis was. They pointed upstairs, so I went straight up to his room, where he lay in bed, wide awake.

'I'm so, so sorry,' I said, as I cradled him in my arms, letting him cry. I sat with him for a long time, not really saying anything, just being there for him. Eventually, I left him with his head buried in a pillow, hoping he would get some sleep.

As I stood up to leave his room, I said, 'I will always be here for you, Lewis, I promise.' I hovered on the threshold and, as I slowly closed the door behind me, I heard him sob deeply. It was a sound that broke my heart.

I went back downstairs to Rich, Nat and my brother Mick, and we sat talking for a long time, trying to make sense of everything. Eventually, we all turned in and I tried to get to sleep, but to no avail. All I could think about was how I was going to tell Ashton, a seven-year-old boy, that his dad was gone forever.

I gave up after a couple of hours and came downstairs to make myself a hot drink. I had just filled the kettle up when Mick, who had stayed the night, walked into the kitchen. I apologised for waking him and he assured me I hadn't, that he hadn't slept either.

After the events of the last twenty-four hours, I felt completely drained, yet I knew there was still so much to do and sort out. Mick offered to help, grabbing a paper and pen and telling me to shout things out as I thought of them so we occupied ourselves with that until it was time for the kids to get up.

It was a while before I heard Ashton's door creak open and my stomach lurched at the thought of what I had to say to him. He walked into the kitchen rubbing sleep from his eyes.

'Can I have my breakfast please, Auntie Jane?' he asked sleepily.

'In a minute, mate,' I replied, trying to keep my voice steady. 'I need to talk to you about something very important first.' I tapped my lap. He climbed on and snuggled into me.

'Ashton,' I began, having to take a few seconds to compose myself. 'You know Daddy has been really poorly and in hospital?'

He nodded, looking into my face.

'Ashton, I'm sorry, sweetheart, but Daddy has died. He has gone to be a twinkle star with Mummy.'

His little face crumpled and he buried his head in my shoulder and sobbed. Mick was sitting at the table, I saw him turn his head away to discreetly wipe away the tears that were falling. I sat holding

Ashton as I had done Lewis the night before and I made him the same promise, 'I'm here for you.' Ashton asked if Lewis knew, and I explained that he did and asked if he wanted to see him, even though he was still in bed. Ashton simply nodded. I carried him up to Lewis's room, where he promptly climbed into bed and cuddled up to his big brother.

With the boys comforting each other upstairs, I turned to my brother for comfort. David and Lisa arrived a few minutes later, and then the stream of visitors, well-wishers, cards and tributes started flooding in, just as they had two years earlier when Gina had been taken. The amount of support was amazing.

Emma was among the visitors that morning. She hadn't been around much in recent months as she had been caring for her granddad who had been very ill, but Rich had texted her after we had rung from the hospital to tell her of Shaun's death, and she really wanted to help in any way she could. She mucked in straight away with domestic jobs, tidying up after the visitors had left and entertaining the little ones.

With Shaun having planned almost everything just a couple of weeks earlier, there weren't too many decisions to be made, but there were still lots of arrangements to organise. I spoke to each of the friends that Shaun had requested would be his pallbearers and they all said they would be honoured. I phoned the funeral director's and asked to speak to Suzanne, but the lovely lady on the other end of the phone explained that Suzanne had moved to the Loughborough branch. By coincidence, the lady I spoke to was from Shepshed herself and had gone to school with Shaun. She promised to get hold of Suzanne and get her to contact me. True to her word Suzanne rang me within the hour, deeply saddened to learn of Shaun's death, and said that she was more than happy to deal with the arrangements. I was relieved as I knew it was what Shaun would have wanted. She reassured me that she would get Shaun home as soon as possible and said she would come out to the house the following afternoon. In the meantime, we continued to try to make arrangements the best we could.

That afternoon I went to visit Ann and Mick, Shaun's parents. They were absolutely devastated and there were no words I could offer to bring them any comfort. I sat holding Ann's hand. Mick just kept repeating that he wished he had put his arms around Shaun as he was taken out to the ambulance on that awful night. The final decline had been so fast, they hadn't had time to visit him in the hospital but, in a way, that may have been a mercy. Ann has since told me that she is glad her memories are of the 'usual Shaun'.

'None of us had expected it to be so quick,' I reassured them. 'There was nothing we could do.'

In truth, I had been questioning myself since the moment he passed away. How could I have not noticed that Shaun was so ill? I know that Shaun was a very proud man and would often hide his pain, but in less than forty-eight hours he had gone from his normal self, laughing and joking with the kids, to not being here at all. The doctors explained pneumonia often meant a rapid decline and I knew the same had happened to my sister, but I was looking for someone to blame, even if it was myself.

Suzanne came out to see us the following afternoon. I asked Lewis if he wanted to join us but he said no, so David, Lisa and I went through the wish list that Shaun had written. Suzanne had also arranged for the vicar to visit us and I was relieved to hear it would be Chris, the same vicar that had conducted Gina's service. As Suzanne left I said, 'Please tell us as soon as he is home.'

She rubbed my arm, as though to comfort me, and replied, 'I promise.'

When Chris came to see us Lewis said he would like to be present, as he knew Chris from services at school and also went to school with his daughter. As before, Chris was warm and kind. We talked about the wish list that Shaun had left and he was more than happy with it but he noted that there were no hymns and asked if we would like any. Before the meeting I had talked this through with various people, including David, and we decided that, although Shaun wasn't religious, it would be appropriate to have 'Swing Low, Sweet Chariot', a hymn that resonates to rugby fans. In fact, when he had renewed his wedding vows to Gina he had led the lads in a chorus of it himself. Chris agreed it was very fitting. As he had done before he said a quiet prayer before he stood to leave.

David, Lisa and I went to The Bottom Railway, the local pub where Shaun had requested his wake be held. The landlord Lee was a personal friend of Shaun's and had played rugby with him for many years. As we sat trying to guess the numbers that would need to be catered for, I had an idea.

'Can we bring his bike in here?' I asked.

The three of them looked at me like I had finally lost the plot. I went on to explain that, rather than have the traditional condolence book we had for

Gina (which I must say holds some lovely words and tributes, and is tucked safely away for the boys when they are older), we could bring his bike and some Post-it notes, so that people could write their personal messages and stick them to his bike. They all thought it was a wonderful idea, so we agreed that is what we would do.

Shaun's brother Andy and I were at David and Lisa's house when I got the call from Suzanne to say that Shaun was 'home'. The news, although welcome, brought on a fresh surge of emotion and we were all in tears again. I knew I had to go over and see Shaun as soon as I could, so I made plans to go over that afternoon.

As I stood outside the little room, waiting to go into the chapel of rest, I had a feeling of déjà vu, remembering the day I stood in the same spot, waiting to see my best friend. Slowly I opened the door and stepped inside, Shaun was dressed in the red T-shirt and jeans that he had requested and he truly looked at peace. His face was relaxed, no longer racked with the tension of putting up with pain, and it really did seem as though he was asleep – like he had dropped off on the sofa after having a big Sunday dinner and a pint or two. I sat with him, held his hand and talked to him for a while.

273

I placed the Livestrong wristband back on his wrist and told him that David would give him his other bracelet back soon. I unclasped his necklace that was hanging around my own neck and put it back around his. As I left I told him that I would see him again soon and placed a kiss on his forehead.

I went back a number of times, as I had with Gina, again because I hated the thought of him being on his own. Plenty of people visited the chapel and most of them went back more than once. Millie decided she would like to say goodbye to Shaun in person. She came with me on one visit and said how very peaceful he looked. She said she was glad (if that's the right word) to have seen him looking so free of pain, and she held his hand and told him how much she missed him – and her Auntie Gina. Both Marco and Lewis had taken the decision that they didn't want to visit, and I accepted that. They each had their own special memories of the last time they had seen him. Those memories were the ones they wanted to keep alive in their heads, and in their hearts.

• • •

On the morning of his funeral I once again laid out the boys' black trousers, white shirts and ties. This time, though, I didn't give them black ties. They each wore a Shepshed Rugby Football Club tie that had belonged to their dad. Lewis got himself ready and I helped Ashton and Anni-Mae to dress. David helped Marco with his tie and Millie fussed over me. Mick and Shaun's auntie Margaret were there with me too and I knew my other brother Rich and my niece Sam would be waiting at the church for us.

As he had requested, I went to see Shaun for one final farewell that morning.

It was hard knowing this would be the last time I would see him. I had had to say goodbye to too many important people in my life, and the memories of burying Gina and my sister Ann were all too fresh in my mind.

Shaun looked the same, as though he was sleeping; I took his hand and told him, once again, that I would love and care for his boys as my own. I asked him to give Gina the biggest hug for me and make sure that she knew how much I missed her. I placed sealed envelopes containing letters from the boys in the coffin with him and a picture that Anni-Mae had drawn, just as she had with Gina, and I smiled as I looked at the rugby ball that David had placed next to him.

Finally, I kissed him on the forehead yet again and said, 'Sleep well, Shaun.'

As I arrived back at the house Lewis was waiting by the front door for me and enveloped me into his arms, so we stood for a while having a cuddle. Then it was time to go.

As the hearse and the funeral cars pulled up outside, I was suddenly overwhelmed with a feeling of panic.

'I can't,' I gasped. 'I can't do this.'

Everyone was really supportive, telling me, 'Take your time. You can do it.'

Luckily, Lewis and Ashton were already standing in the hallway with Marco, Millie and Anni-Mae so they couldn't see me panic. I knew I had to pull myself together, if only for the sake of the boys, so I took a deep breath and walked out to them, taking a small hand in each of my own as we walked up the drive, all of us looking at the floor. I helped the little ones with their seatbelts, and turned in my seat to offer my hand to each of the older ones in the seat behind me. I squeezed each of their hands in turn, and then the cars pulled slowly away.

After travelling to church in the two cars, seated as Shaun had requested, we were met by the pallbearers. I knew the church was already packed to the rafters as there were a number of well-wishers standing outside as they couldn't fit in. I stood in the middle of Ashton and Anni-Mae, one of their little hands in each of mine. Lewis, Marco and Millie would walk behind us. As we were just about to walk through the church doors, I turned to see that Marco and Millie had each taken one of Lewis's hands in theirs. Our families' lives had been brought together by friendship and love, and forced together by tragedy, and yet in the midst of our sadness we were united as one. I was so proud of them all that I can't even find the words to describe it.

We walked into church to the strains of the familiar Starship song. Shaun had chosen to enter church to the song that was special to him and Gina, the same one he had played at her funeral: 'Nothing's Gonna Stop Us Now'. My eye drifted to the sea of colour – the motocross riders had all worn their race shirts, as before.

The vicar gave a moving speech, and then it was time for the tributes and I was up first. I talked of Shaun's strength and courage, and how inspirational he was. I talked of his love for Gina and his two wonderful boys and what a privilege it had been to have spent so much time with him since Gina's death. I then renewed the promise I had made to Gina at her funeral, only this time I made a promise to both of them, that I would love and care for Lewis and Ashton always, as if they were my own. Again

I meant every word from the bottom of my heart. I looked at the boys as I made this vow. Ashton was looking at the floor and clutching Lewis's hand, but Lewis looked back at me and slowly nodded his head, as if to say, 'I know you will.'

As before, I struggled to keep my emotions in check. This time, it was Shaun's brother David who stood beside me, offering support.

After me, Phil stood up and read his own tribute, very touching and moving, but sprinkled with a little of that Shaun-style humour. Then the organ started for 'Swing Low, Sweet Chariot', the vicar encouraged all the rugby players to find their voices, and boy did they do just that! We then all sat in silence as the second song Shaun chose, John Lennon's haunting ballad 'Imagine', was played.

The vicar wound up the service and, as we stood to follow Shaun's coffin back out of the church, a tearful chuckle rippled through the congregation. Shaun had chosen Monty Python's 'Always Look on the Bright Side of Life' as his final song. I couldn't help but smile to myself. And that was exactly the reaction he had been hoping for.

The close family and friends who would be at the burial made our way to the same plot in which we had buried Gina, just two years before. As Shaun was lowered into the ground, the children, other family members and I each threw in a white rose. I copied Shaun's final gesture for Gina by placing a kiss on the rose before tossing it in, and the five children took my lead and did the same.

I was worried what the little ones would make of the burial. I had always told them that people we loved went to heaven when they died, that they were 'angels on the twinkle stars', yet they were going to witness a coffin being lowered into the ground, With this in mind I had ordered some orange helium balloons (orange being the colour of Shaun's KTM motocross bike), and close friends and family were each given a card to write a message on, which would then be attached to the balloons before they were released. The children loved that idea because as far as they were concerned the balloons would go up and up until they reached the stars and heaven. As Suzanne carried them to the graveside, the bold colour somehow gave a glimmer of hope and releasing them to the skies was a poignant and beautiful moment. However, it didn't quite go as smoothly as planned as the strings had become tangled in the back of the car, I remember thinking that Gina and Shaun would both have seen the funny side of that. But with a bit of patience and tugging they rose into the sky. I looked around at the flowers and, again, I was amazed by the number. At Gina's funeral there had been an array of pinks. Now, for Shaun, there was every shade of orange.

We left the cemetery and went to join all the other mourners at the wake. I did as expected and mingled, making sure all the kids were never out of my sight. Ashton was soon running around, grabbing a bite to eat every time he passed by the food table. Lewis was a lot more sombre though. He looked as though his heart was heavy but whenever I looked for him, Marco and Millie were by his side, as though they were protecting him. On that sad day the love those five children have for each other was clear for everyone to see.

As the evening wore on the tears stopped and the laughter came, the crowd getting ever rowdier.

'Good,' I remember thinking. 'Shaun has got his last wish of "a bloody good piss up".'

Back at home, with the kids tucked safely in bed, I sat talking to Shaun's auntie Margaret, who had offered to stay with us for the night, then lay awake long into the dark hours thinking of Gina, Shaun and the future of their two beautiful boys.

I knew that tomorrow would be the start of a whole new chapter of our lives.

CHAPTER 12

A NEW BEGINNING

In the days after the funeral, it was a struggle to get through everyday chores and bring some sort of normality into our devastated lives. The all-consuming emptiness, the bitterness and the anger that I had felt when Gina died returned. It felt like everyone else's world was still turning, but for this little family it had stopped. But looking at the faces of the children made me determined to turn these negative emotions into positive ones.

The boys appeared to cope remarkably well, for the most part, and that gave me strength. My brothers, David and Lisa, my niece Sam, my friends Julie, David and Sally, and many other family members and friends rallied round, and they still do to this day. They are an amazing help and I couldn't have got through it without them.

On the Sunday after Shaun's death, we attended a Shepshed Rugby Football Club game and, once again, there was a minute's silence before the match. The boys each took one of my hands and stood with their heads bowed. Ashton shed a few tears, but Lewis tried to be the man and stay strong, though to me it was obvious that he wanted to break down. He did himself proud.

Afterwards they gave us the match ball with 'Buster' – Shaun's nickname – written across it. Sometime after the funeral, they held another match between the current players and the old boys' team, which would have included Shaun. They had a trophy engraved with Shaun's name and asked me and the boys to attend and present the trophy to the winning team, which we were honoured to do.

Lewis was really impressed when he saw the trophy. 'Dad would loved that,' he said. Both the boys shouted and cheered their way through the match and, afterwards, all three off us went up to present the trophy.

Like his dad, Lewis is a keen rugby player, playing for Loughborough, so we can all very often be found on the side of a wet muddy field on a Sunday morning, shouting words of encouragement. Lewis even went on tour with his team, and David went with him as the responsible adult. Lewis had laughed, joking, 'Who will be looking after who?'

Lewis, being a typical teenage boy, didn't like showing his feelings too much in the months after Shaun's death, but every now and again he would confide in me that he was having a bad day. For the most part this meant that he just needed time on his own, but occasionally what he wanted more than anything was a cuddle and I was more than happy to oblige. Sitting quietly with him in my arms was the least I could do for this very special boy.

Ashton went through a stage of waking in the night, crying for his mum and dad, which was heartbreaking. I would lie with him and remind him of something good they had all done together We would talk about holidays, Christmases, Daddy laughing at Mummy's cooking, Daddy falling off his motocross bike, Mummy's silly singing and dancing, anything that would make him smile. Then I would sit and stroke his hair until he drifted back to sleep. I even sprayed one of his teddy bears with Shaun's aftershave and he would fall asleep with the teddy nestled under his nose, with happy thoughts of his dad.

Marco and Millie were like a rock to me and the boys. Only young adults, but still my babies, they never failed to support me, the boys and Anni-Mae. Christmas was fast approaching and I was dreading it, but they got me into the Christmas spirit, reminding me when I simply couldn't face it that we had to make it as good as possible for Lewis and Ashton. I arrived home one day to find they had got the Christmas tree out and were decorating it. I couldn't help but smile, I was so proud.

Determined to make it a good Christmas, we all set about with the planning, with the kids writing Christmas lists and me doing the shopping. Christmas is one of the times that I miss Gina the most, but I decided the best gift I could give to her, and to Shaun, was to make sure that we all had a great Christmas together.

It was around this time that Lewis and some of his friends decided that they wanted to get involved in some fundraising for Cancer Research. Lewis dressed up as Father Christmas and his friends from his tutor group dressed as Santa's Little Helpers, and they sold candy canes around school. The local paper got in touch and Lewis even got to do a live radio interview with his friends and form tutor. He explained that he remembered all the fundraising his mum and dad had done after Shaun's diagnosis and he too wanted to give something back.

The Christmas collection went so well that they did the same the following Valentine's Day, with Lewis dressed as James Bond, selling chocolate hearts, and then again at Easter, selling chocolate eggs dressed as Easter Bunnies! I am so proud of Lewis and his friends. So far they have raised over £1,500 and their efforts soon came to the attention of the organisation Giving Nation, which encourages young people to put time and effort into helping others. They were all invited to London for the Giving Nation Awards and, after a whistle-stop tour of the city and a ride on the London Eye, they went to the award ceremony at Her Majesty's Treasury. Lewis was really excited that evening as he told me the room where they had received the award was the room where Winston Churchill made several war time broadcasts. They had to prepare a short speech and Lewis admitted he was terrified when he stood to say his share of the words. He was impressed by the other schools and what they had been doing for their fundraising.

When Lewis arrived home that evening he was grinning from ear to ear, a framed certificate in his hand. Shepshed High School had won the

Fundraising Award at the ceremony. I was elated for him. They had worked hard and they deserved the recognition.

'Yes! Well done, mate,' I said giving him a hug. 'Your mum and dad would be so proud.'

But I didn't really need to tell him that, because he knew it already.

• • •

That December, it was the first Christmas when Marco could legally drink, as he was now 18, so I wasn't surprised when he said he would like to go to a party on Christmas Eve. I agreed I would pick him up later that night. With the little ones fast asleep, I left Millie and Lewis engrossed in something on the TV, both with their hands buried in the tin of Christmas sweets that was wedged between them on the sofa, and headed off to collect Marco. A little worse for wear, he kept telling me all the way home that he loved me and was proud of me, which made me laugh as he's emotional enough without alcohol. Lewis and Millie thought it was hilarious as he wobbled through the door when we got back.

We sat for a short while then decided to head up to bed. Marco was sleeping in Lewis's room with him. 'Good luck!' I joked as we walked into Lewis's room. I gave them both a hug and kiss and left as

Lewis tried to help Marco out of his shoes and up the ladder into the bunk bed. I really couldn't help chuckling to myself as I heard Marco slurring, 'I love you, Lewis. As far as I'm concerned you're my brother, you know.'

'I love you too, Marco, now please just get into bed,' Lewis replied, giggling.

'Careful, bro, don't drop me,' came the muffled voice of Marco. I popped my head back round the door to see Marco's head buried in the pillow as Lewis gave him a leg up.

This little incident comes up in conversation regularly. 'Am I stuck with Marco again this Christmas Eve?' Lewis joked recently.

'No,' I replied. 'We can just dump him on the sofa.'

'No, he can come in with me really,' laughed Lewis.

It's good entertainment. As it turned out, we had a great Christmas, all things considered. It wasn't as magical as the year before, Shaun's last Christmas, when Shaun had dressed in a Santa suit and pretended to have snooze in the chair so that when Anni-Mae and Ashton had run in to see if Santa had been, they thought Santa had fallen sleep in their house.

We reminisced about that as we opened our presents on this Christmas morning, the little ones happily reliving the memory. Lewis, Marco and Millie laughed about how Gina and I used to be more excited than the children and they said they had never known anyone else go Christmas shopping as much as the two of us did. After we opened the presents and the younger ones had played for a while, and I'd finished the final preparations for dinner, we all went together to the cemetery to see Gina and Shaun, the little ones falling over their words as they talked about presents they had received.

Upholding the Hibberd family tradition, we trooped to the pub for half an hour with Shaun's family. Then it was home for a three-course Christmas dinner, which we followed by playing new board games, building Lego, playing with new dolls and lots more festive fun. The kids were exhausted by the time they flopped into bed that night. The older three and I sat eating Christmas chocolates and watching TV till it was very late.

As I lay in bed that night I smiled to myself. We had done it: we had made it a great Christmas. Gina and Shaun would have approved.

• • •

With five children and two houses to look after, life today is constantly busy, but I wouldn't change it for the world – unless it meant we could have Gina and Shaun back. But we can't, so I am determined to make the most of what we do have – each other.

Shaun's family have taken myself and my children on as family, and likewise my family have Lewis and Ashton. Whenever there is a birthday or any other event we are seen by everyone as Jane and the five children. It's heart-warming that people have accepted we are one big family now; heart-warming and comforting, and I know from speaking to all the children they feel that way too.

One of the things I love so much about the children is that they are all so close, yet they have such very different characteristics.

Marco is the joker, he is very funny and witty. It's hard to be sad and down when he is around because there is always a little comment or gesture that brings a smile to your face, but he is very sensitive and worries about me and his brothers and sisters constantly.

Millie is beautiful and intelligent. She is also ambitious and can be opinionated when she wants to be, standing up for anything that she believes in.

Family and friends are the most important thing in the world to her, alongside her dog, JJ.

Lewis is incredibly sporty, a keen rugby player like his dad. Like his dad, he is also funny at times, and at others he becomes a serious young man. I feel sad that in some ways he has had to grow up so quickly but he is a credit to his mum and dad, a loving lad, who doesn't give up on anything easily.

Ashton is comical and has us all laughing, if not always intentionally. I often say he is like a little old man, though he is very innocent in the daft comments he comes out with. He often speaks without thinking, but is the first to laugh at himself when he realises what he has said. He has a wicked imagination and he is a very loving little boy who adores his cuddles.

Last but not least is Anni-Mae, the baby of our family, who is very strong-willed and knows her own mind – and I have to say she can come across as determined at times! But she is very creative, always sticking and gluing and creating things. She, like Ashton, loves her cuddles, and she is a very kind-hearted little girl who loves to look after others; I'm proud that a number of teachers have commented about her lovely caring nature.

Together they make a rowdy bunch and the house is never quiet when they are around, but I wouldn't change a thing about any of them.

Lewis and Ashton both carry a lot of traits from their mum and dad. They are both the spitting image of Gina, so I love looking at them and seeing so much of her in them. Like their mum they are strong-willed, outgoing and live life to the full. Like their dad they are both sporty with strong personalities. Gina and Shaun definitely live on inside those two boys.

• • •

After some discussion with Lewis we recently decided to get a puppy and, having researched the breeds, we chose a puggle – a cross between a pug and a beagle. Anni-Mae's and Ashton's faces were a picture when they came out of school to see the little bundle wrapped in a blanket. They were besotted with our new arrival.

We chose the name Angel for her. A couple of days after she arrived Ashton made us all laugh when he announced, 'Angel's trumped and she smells just like Dad!' He wasn't saying it with any malice, just in a matter-of-fact way, and it made us all giggle.

There always seems to be something going on, with sports, after-school clubs and so on. Birthdays seem to come around quickly, with five to think about. This year Ashton chose to have a bowling party and great fun was had by everyone. It was fantastic to see Lewis and Ashton laughing together, especially during Ashton's turn when he let go of the bowling ball too soon, just as he swung it behind him, and nearly took out the crowd of mums and dads standing behind us. If that wasn't enough, a couple of turns later he let go too late and went flying down the lane at the same time as the ball!

I took the children to Butlins in Skegness for a family holiday this year. Marco couldn't join us because of work commitments. I was disappointed, but I have to accept he is a young man now. I allowed Millie and Lewis to take a friend each, and my friend Hayley joined us to keep me company, so in total there were eight of us. It was absolutely manic, but we had a wonderful time and everyone got along really well. It was lovely to see all the kids united. Without a shadow of a doubt we looked like one big happy family and in my eyes that's just what we are!

Lewis and Ashton have adjusted so well, they are both as happy as they can be and settled at school, as are my two girls. Marco, at nearly 20, is his own man, and worries about me as much as I worry about him.

Both Lewis's and Ashton's schools were incredibly supportive throughout everything, but it was still difficult when I attended the first parents' evenings as the boys' legal guardian. The other children sat with their mum or dad, or both, and this made me feel angry, yet again. It should have been Gina and Shaun sitting there, hearing the teachers praise their boys, not me. I love the boys so much but the unfairness of it all does still get to me, especially at events like that.

At the end of June, Lewis left Shepshed High School to take up a place at college and the school held a prom. Lewis has some really good friends and they were determined to arrive in style, but not in a limousine, not even in a sports car. For weeks before the prom the four of them worked together to make a life-size Flintstones car out of papier mâché. Kane's mum made simple costumes to put over their suits and, as they ran along with their feet poking from the bottom of their prehistoric vehicle, she drove behind them with The Flintstones music blaring from the car. Despite the number of high-powered cars, limousines, trucks and even a JCB digger, they were the star attraction.

Needless to say they won the prize for the best arrival.

I could almost hear Gina's infectious laugh ringing out as I imagined how she'd have encouraged Lewis's crazy ideas. She would have loved to have seen him that night.

• • •

One afternoon in May 2013, my phone rang and a female voice said, 'My name's Nikki and I'm calling from the *Leicester Mercury*.'

That didn't strike me as particularly unusual. I had had local reporters ringing before because of the various fundraising events I'd been involved in since Shaun was diagnosed and other charity events that friends had taken part in, since his death, in aid of LOROS. Lewis's fundraising also meant that papers had recently been in touch for permission to print stories about him and I assumed this was a similar call.

'Do you know your daughter entered you into the Mum of the Year award?' continued Nikki.

'You what?' was all I could say. I was stunned.

'Your daughter Amelia?' she said, because Millie had used her full name for the form. 'She entered you for the Mum of the Year award.'

'Oh,' I said.

Nikki was laughing now, but she went on, 'We've been overwhelmed with entries but I'm pleased to tell you, you're in the final eight. Are you free on the 27th of June?'

'I don't know. Why?' I replied.

'You need to be at the champagne award ceremony. Give me your email address and I'll send you a copy of what your daughter wrote. I have to say, she's a beautiful writer.'

True to her word, Nikki sent over a copy of what Millie had sent. I was absolutely sobbing by the time I'd finished reading it.

My mum should be mum of the year for lots of reasons but mainly because since 2009 she has been an inspiration. In 2009, a great family friend was diagnosed with lung cancer, his name is Shaun Hibberd and he was just 36 years old. He was my little sister's godfather and I had always called him Uncle. His wife Gina Hibberd was my mum's best friend and was like my auntie.

The news hit everyone like a brick, but my mum kept everyone strong, including me, my brother Marco, my little sister Anni-Mae, Shaun, Gina and their two children Lewis and Ashton, visiting Shaun in hospital, caring for Lewis and Ashton, always being there for Gina to scream at or just cry, as well as helping with lots of fundraising for the Roy Castle Lung Cancer Foundation. As Shaun's cancer spread another tragedy got to us all, as on 12 October Gina Hibberd was killed in a car crash.

As you can imagine Shaun and his children, along with my mum, myself and my brother and sister were heartbroken. Things got very difficult for us all but again my mum was always there for all of us throughout this tough time, from helping to arrange the funeral to making phone calls or just being a rock to everyone. Shaun gradually got worse and my mum attended all hospital appointments with him and sat with him during his chemotherapy, cared for him and his boys as well as us when the treatment made him sick, and supported Shaun as he was on a roller coaster of emotions. The cancer continued to spread around his body and my mum never left his side, giving up work to care for him and us, we could all see Shaun getting weaker and I heard my mum crying but she never let the brave face drop to myself and the other kids.

When Shaun had to start spending time in LOROS my mum's brave face started to fade. She didn't go out and hardly saw anyone apart from us all. She very often stayed in LOROS with Shaun *so that he didn't feel alone or frightened. As Shaun got worse he was worrying about his two boys, Lewis and Ashton, as they knew he was dying but thought their mum Gina would still be there to care for them, but this was no longer the case. Shaun asked my mum if she would take care of Lewis and Ashton and after checking with us she agreed to take on the role of mum and dad for them when the time came. Shaun arranged for a court hearing so that it was all formal that my mum would be their legal guardian so that Shaun could have some peace of mind.*

Shaun passed away on 5 November with my mum at his bedside holding his hand. He had fought his battle with cancer so bravely with my mum never leaving him, and him knowing that she would love Lewis and Ashton as her own! She is now caring for me Millie Plume (16) Marco Plume (19) Lewis Hibberd (14) Ashton Hibberd (7) and my little sister Anni-Mae Richardson (7) and she is doing an AMAZING job! That's why my mum should be Mum of the Year, she never puts herself first! Thank you for reading.

Millie Plume.'

From the many entries, the reporter had narrowed it down to sixty and then an independent panel of judges had picked the eight finalists, including the two runners-up and the overall winner. Before the ceremony, I had to go to the *Leicester Mercury* offices where they took pictures of me and Millie, which went in the paper on the Tuesday, two days before the ceremony, with a bit of a write-up.

I was allowed to bring five people to the award ceremony, so I took Marco, Millie and Lewis – not Anni-Mae and Ashton because they would have been bored within ten minutes. Lisa also came along because she is now a really close friend.

As it was a formal event, I bought a sleeveless cream dress with flowers embroidered up the front for the ceremony and Millie wore a sleeveless ivory dress. As Millie and I walked down the stairs Lisa, who was waiting in the hallway, shed a few tears as she told us that we both looked beautiful.

The awards were held at the City Rooms in Leicester and it was all very grand. We were met at the door and given champagne, taken to a reception area where people were having a drink and chatting, and a photographer from the paper was taking pictures. Former badminton champion Gail Emms, who had just had a baby, was the guest speaker and she came over and spoke to each of the finalists, then we went upstairs. Gail gave a moving speech, where she said, 'When people ask me who I most want to be, I say, "It's simple. My mum. My mum got me where I am today."' It was lovely.

Over a beautiful three-course meal, I read all the other finalists' stories and began thinking, 'Why me? I've not done anything special.' There were some incredible stories. But Lisa said, 'If you read them, they are amazing, but they are all things mums have done for their own children. You have done all you have done for two boys who aren't yours.'

'But Gina would have done exactly the same for me,' I argued. 'It's nothing special.'

During the meal, Marco went down to the bar to get himself a drink and, when he came back, he sat down without a word just as they started to announce the winners. Before they named each one, they read part of the nomination that had been sent in and I was sobbing at every one – so were Lisa and Millie. Lewis and Marco were looking at us like we were bonkers!

They announced third place – a wonderful foster mum – and she went to the stage to get her big bouquet and goodie bag, then they announced second place, who was a mum of two, battling leukaemia. 'I thought she'd have won,' I said to Marco.

'Hmmm', he said enigmatically.

I looked back at the booklet with the stories in and pointed at another finalist. 'I think she's going to win,' I said.

'Yeah, I do,' agreed Marco, with no emotion on his face.

Then Amanda Phillips, the manager of the Leicester shopping centre that sponsored the event, said, 'I'm so pleased to announce that the winner of Mum of the Year 2013 is Jane Plume.'

My mouth fell open. Lisa screamed and burst into tears. Marco said, 'Come on, Mum. You've got to get up and go onstage.' I was so shocked I found it really hard to walk up on to the stage. I couldn't say anything because I was actually speechless. They handed me a trophy and flowers, but I could hardly carry them. I was a nervous wreck. I got back to the table and Lewis was absolutely sobbing. I went straight to him and put my arms round him and he kept saying, 'You're the best. You're the best. I love you.' My heart was in my mouth as I hugged him. Lisa was crying, Millie was crying so I gave her a cuddle and she said, 'I love you so much, Mum.' Then I turned round to look at Marco and he had a big smirk on his face.

'You don't seem very surprised,' I said.

'I knew,' he laughed.

'What do you mean, you knew?' I asked.

Apparently, when he'd gone down to the bar to get a drink, he'd seen them unwrapping the trophy with my name on it, so he knew I had got something, but he didn't know whether I'd actually won until they announced the runners-up. He didn't let on when he got back to the table. He didn't even smirk at me so I had no idea – but it meant he could keep his composure while the rest of us fell apart.

'If I hadn't have known I would have blubbered like a baby,' he admitted to me later, and he did go to pieces when we got home, although he'll kill me for sharing that.

After I picked up the award everything went crazy, with people asking for interviews, pictures. All of the six judges came over to speak to me personally and complimented Millie's writing. All of them, even the two male judges said, 'She had me in tears.'

The Mum of the Year awards finished at three and then I had to go straight from Leicester to Melton Mowbray for Millie's graduation, where she was awarded a distinction and named Student of the Year. It was a very emotional day. I spent all day crying!

• • •

With the summer over, the anniversary of Shaun's death in November loomed on the horizon. It felt like it was coming for a long time, maybe because it's the anniversary of my own dad's death the day before. This gave me so much empathy for the boys. My dad had been gone for twenty-five years, and I'm an adult, but I still find that day incredibly hard. It helped me to imagine just a little of what Lewis and Ashton were going to be feeling, but it was just one year on and they were children, and they hadn't got their mum to comfort them.

I spoke to Lewis about how he might want to mark the date. He said he wanted to keep the day low key, so we visited the cemetery together, and spoke about Shaun and Gina a lot throughout the day. The rest of the time I just allowed the boys the freedom to be lost in their own thoughts. For my part, it was a chance to reflect on the precious friends I have lost – but also the precious gift of their children, and how our little family is adapting as the months go by.

When we lost Gina and then Shaun, I vowed to love Lewis and Ashton as my own – and I do. I treat all five of them the same, I kiss and cuddle them all, I tell them I love them and how proud I am of them

– and I tell them off if they play up or don't do their homework.

Lewis and Ashton are doing well at school and the kids all get on brilliantly. They argue occasionally, yes, but what siblings don't? Earlier this year, Lewis asked for some money to get birthday cards for Millie and Marco. When he returned from the shop, he had brought brother and sister cards, which really moved me.

We talk about Gina and Shaun all the time. The house is full of photos of them, but we still regularly pull out other photographs to look through as well. I am so lucky to have had two such wonderful people in my life, and so glad that I have my own special memories to share with the children. Everyone has stories about them. Gina's sister Keri tells us tales of when Gina was a child and teenager, before I had the pleasure of meeting her. I am determined that the boys will grow up remembering how wonderful and special their mum and dad were.

At six foot three, Lewis is getting too big for me to kiss him goodnight, but I manage to sneak one in occasionally. As I tuck Ashton in, I always kiss him three times, one from Mummy, one from Daddy and one from me.

There isn't a day goes by that Lewis and Ashton don't miss their mum and dad. It tears me apart to think of those special moments in the boys' lives that their parents will miss – the birthdays, graduations, first jobs, weddings and even the births of their own children one day in the future. At the same time there isn't a day when I don't miss my special friends, and Marco, Millie and Anni-Mae their Auntie Gina and Uncle Shaun. They live on inside our hearts and always will. Marco even has a tattoo for each of them in their memory. He has 'Gina, heaven needed an angel and took someone perfect' across his shoulders and, for Shaun, a rugby ball with 'Buster' written across it and '173', Shaun's motocross race number.

Some people may have found it hard, living here, in their house, now that they are both gone, but I love being in the house they shared because there are so many happy memories here for Lewis, Ashton, me and my children. If I close my eyes I can hear the laughter and hustle and bustle of the times when Gina and Shaun were still here. To me this is their home. In fact I still say if someone asks where I am going 'over to Gina and Shaun's'.

When night-time falls and the stars are twinkling in the sky, Anni-Mae and Ashton often have a competition to find the brightest star. Ashton sometimes points at the sky and excitedly exclaims, 'Auntie Jane, Auntie Jane, I've found Mummy and Daddy's star. Up there, look. That's the brightest one so that's where the best angels are!'

'You're right there, mate,' I will say. He will then wave and blow a kiss up into the night sky.

Lewis often jokes, 'I bet they're causing a riot up there!'

Even David and Lisa carry this on with their own children. At bedtime Lisa sings 'Twinkle Twinkle Auntie Gina's Star' or 'Uncle Shaun's Star'. Their youngest child, Dylan, never even met Gina and Shaun but if you show him a picture he can name them immediately.

I hope my friends *are* causing a riot up there, that they are happy together and watching over us. They trusted me with their greatest treasures in their two boys. I hope I'm making them proud.

The question I get asked most often is why? Why did I put my life on hold to nurse Shaun? Why did I take on someone else's children when I already had three of my own?

The answer is simple: 'Gina would have done the same for me.'

AUTHOR'S NOTE

I have to confess I was somewhat overwhelmed when the opportunity came up to write this book. But the more I thought about it, the more I wanted to do it. I wanted the facts to be put down on paper for Lewis and Ashton and any future family they might have, and I wanted them, and the whole world, to know what wonderful people their parents were.

I couldn't think of a better way to pay tribute to the wonderful friend that Gina was. Naturally, I discussed the book with all five of the children before agreeing to go ahead. Anni-Mae and Ashton don't really understand, but were very excited about a book being written with their names in. Lewis,

Marco and Millie all had the same reaction: 'Go for it!' Getting the backing from them was all I needed. I spoke to other family members and friends who all thought it was a lovely idea and said they would support me. It has been heart-wrenching at times I admit, but in some ways therapeutic, helping to bring to the fore of my mind all the happy memories that grief somehow locks away.

Lisa, Hayley and Gina's sister Keri have all said to me that Gina would have loved the thought of a book being written about her. She would have laughed her socks off and danced around, crowing, 'Oh yes, get me. That book is all about me!' They are absolutely right.

I hope she would have liked it. I hope I've done her proud.

Gina – this is for you.

ACKNOWLEDGEMENTS

Thank you to the angels. The biggest thank you I want to dedicate is to Gina and Shaun, you trusted me with the most precious gifts ever – your wonderful boys. My mum and dad, for bringing me up to be the person I am today and instilling in me the importance of the love of a family. My sister, just for being my big sister.

Marco and Millie for the maturity they showed when their lives were turned upside down, I couldn't be more proud of the amazing young man and young lady you have become. Anni-Mae, my own little princess. I love you all so much.

Lewis and Ashton, I love you both with all my heart, you are both incredibly strong and I hope you are as proud of yourselves as I am of you!

So many others that I want to thank. My brother

Mick, for always being there, telling it how it is, and in so many ways being my mum and dad, along with my brother Rich and sister-in-law Michele. Again, always being there whenever I need you, even when at times I didn't realise just how much. My nieces and nephews, I love all of you as though you were my own children. To my niece Sam, one of my best friends who has held me as I cried, listened as I've moaned, and endlessly helped me with the practical things, just when I've needed it. Thank you to you all for accepting Lewis and Ashton into our family with open arms and open hearts. I honestly don't know how I would do it without you. I love you all!

To Shaun's family, who have in turn welcomed me and my children into their own family. His mum and dad, Ann and Mick, who are always there to lend a hand with the countless lifts to rugby, or pick up from school. David and Lisa: where would I be without you? I have gained two more people into my life as best friends, always there for any of us. I love you.

Keri and Mike: Lewis and Ashton know they have a connection with their mum in you, that in itself means the world.

I am blessed to have so many wonderful friends in my life, at times we don't get to see each other as often as we would like, but we know that we are always there for each other. Special thanks to Hayley, not only for being an amazing, loving understanding friend, but for introducing me to the most special lady, Gina. Julie 'Ju Ju', no matter what life has thrown at you, you have always been there for me and my children, at the most difficult times in my life, no words can convey what that means to me and I cannot give enough thanks! David and Sally for keeping me grounded when things have been tough – thank you for being such good friends. Emma, Kaz, Moira, Ann and Stuart along with other friends and family – sorry if I haven't mentioned you personally, but you have all contributed in some way and I can never thank you enough.

I have to say a massive thank you to Alison Maloney, for the countless emails, reassurance when I was panicking, and for being a genuinely nice person, so easy to talk to. I have enjoyed working with you immensely, you're a star! To Kate, I wouldn't have done this without you, thank you for believing in me in the first place.